June 2013 – DWP

NCTE's Theory and Research into Practice (TRIP) series presents volumes of works designed to offer a teacher audience a solid theoretical foundation in a given subject area within English language arts, exposure to the pertinent research in that area, and a number of practice-oriented models designed to stimulate theory-based application in the reader's own classroom.

Volumes Currently Available in the Series

360 Degrees of Text: Using Poetry to Teach Close Reading and Powerful Writing (2011), Eileen Murphy Buckley

Writing about Literature, Second Edition, Revised and Updated (2009), Larry R. Johannessen, Elizabeth A. Kahn, and Carolyn Calhoun Walter

Middle Ground: Exploring Selected Literature from and about the Middle East (2008), Sheryl L. Finkle and Tamara J. Lilly

Genre Theory: Teaching, Writing, and Being (2008), Deborah Dean

Code-Switching: Teaching Standard English in Urban Classrooms (2006), Rebecca S. Wheeler and Rachel Swords

Computers in the Writing Classroom (2002), Dave Moeller

Co-Authoring in the Classroom: Creating an Environment for Effective Collaboration (1997), Helen Dale

Beyond the "SP" Label: Improving the Spelling of Learning Disabled Writers (1992), Patricia J. McAlexander, Ann B. Dobie, and Noel Gregg

Illumination Rounds: Teaching the Literature of the Vietnam War (1992), Larry R. Johannessen

Unlocking Shakespeare's Language: Help for the Teacher and Student (1988), Randal Robinson

Explorations: Introductory Activities for Literature and Composition, 7–12 (1987), Peter Smagorinsky, Tom McCann, and Stephen Kern

Writing about Literature (1984), Elizabeth Kahn, Carolyn Calhoun Walter, and Larry R. Johannessen

Learning to Spell (1981), Richard E. Hodges

360 Degrees of Text

Using Poetry to Teach Close Reading and Powerful Writing

Eileen Murphy Buckley
Chicago Public Schools

National Council of Teachers of English
1111 W. Kenyon Road, Urbana, Illinois 61801-1096

Yusef Komunyakaa, "Facing It" from *Pleasure Dome: New and Collected Poems* © 2001 by Yusef Komunyakaa. Reprinted with permission of Wesleyan University Press.

Manuscript Editor: Jane M. Curran

Production Editor: Bonny Graham

Interior Design: Doug Burnett

Cover Design: Pat Mayer

Cover Image: iStockphoto.com/Raycat

NCTE Stock Number: 60237

It is the policy of NCTE in its journals and other publications to provide a forum for the open discussion of ideas concerning the content and the teaching of English and the language arts. Publicity accorded to any particular point of view does not imply endorsement by the Executive Committee, the Board of Directors, or the membership at large, except in announcements of policy, where such endorsement is clearly specified.

Every effort has been made to provide current URLs and email addresses, but because of the rapidly changing nature of the Web, some sites and addresses may no longer be accessible.

Library of Congress Cataloging-in-Publication Data

Buckley, Eileen Murphy, 1970–
    360 degrees of text : using poetry to teach close reading and powerful writing / Eileen Murphy Buckley.
        p. cm. — (Theory and research into practice (TRIP) series)
    Includes bibliographical references and index.
    ISBN 978-0-8141-6023-7 ((pbk))
    1. Language arts (Elementary) 2. Language arts (Secondary) 3. Language experience approach in education. 4. Children—Language. I. National Council of Teachers of English. II. Title. III. Title: Three hundred sixty degrees of text. IV. Title: Three hundred and sixty degrees of text.
    LB1576.B8825 2011
    372.6'044—dc23
                                                                    2011033374

For every student, teacher, writer, and performer who has made being mortal worth it, at least for me. Also, for my family, especially my father, an untamed idealist, and my mother, a practical dreamer, both of whom fueled my imagination. For my husband, Michael, who is my best friend and my best editor. And finally, for my children, Michael, Darragh, Orlaith, and Enya, who humble me daily with this reminder: we must revere the life of the mind.

Contents

Introduction

The theory behind the 360-degree approach I advocate in this book is drawn from research on the best practices in the several areas of the English language arts field and from my own work as a student of my students. At the core of all this research is the argument that <u>students</u> can <u>gain</u> <u>textual power</u> <u>across genres</u> when <u>they engage</u> in <u>increasingly</u> <u>rigorous tasks</u> with <u>increasingly</u> <u>rigorous texts.</u> But the only way we can lead them through the process of becoming closer readers and more powerful writers is by engaging them from the inside out with the power of ideas and many fruitful experiences with skilled reading and writing.

The first part of the book addresses the theoretical backing of my approach. In addition to providing some insight into the research that influenced this work, I attempted to answer a range of key questions I encounter when talking with others about what I now call the 360-degree approach.

Part 2 of the book comprises three chapters, each providing specific practical lessons for implementing the 360-degree approach. In Chapter 2, "Teaching Close Reading through Performance and Recitation," teachers learn how to engage students in sophisticated close reading activities ranging from visualization to paraphrase so that students learn to get the gist of a poem by capitalizing on the interpretive powers of the mind's eye and their own voices and bodies. The culminating lesson provides a sample of how teachers can help individual students engage more deeply with texts through recitation, a method of extending a poem study that I encourage throughout the remainder of the lessons. These performance-based lessons also lay the groundwork for understanding author's craft through the lens of genre knowledge, which is explored in greater depth in Chapter 3.

Chapter 3, "Teaching Close Reading and Powerful Writing through Imitation," illustrates how teachers can help students explore the choices of poets and to exercise authorial choice themselves by imitating the choices of great writers. Using free verse forms, the hymn, and the ever-popular sonnet as examples of how to teach poetic forms and techniques, teachers will see how useful good old-fashioned imitation can be for helping their apprentices become better readers and writers for academic as well as artistic purposes.

Each imitative writing lesson provides practice with workshop techniques as well. Building on the metacognitive awareness developed through the Think-Aloud activities, the Workshop Templates introduced in this chapter lay the groundwork for academic writing and workshops among peers.

The set of lessons in Chapter 4, "Representing Close Readings in Academic Writing," illustrates how teachers can help students use strategies from earlier chapters to enter a sophisticated reading of the text through its verbs and other sentence parts, while introducing related ideas for instructing students in making claims in explications. The academic writing component moves students through the process of developing summaries and claims to supporting them with coherent, evidence-laden paragraphs. In the last lessons of the chapter, students learn to revise for more powerful sentences and paragraphs.

Since each of these poems raises a number of debatable issues about "big ideas," I have also included a number of curricular debate suggestions for extending each lesson as well. These prompts can act as segues to exploring other genres, thereby helping students see more explicitly how they might apply the textual power they have acquired in their study of poetry to creating evidence-based arguments about all kinds of texts, including nonfiction texts.

At the end of Chapters 2, 3, and 4, I suggest additional resources. In addition to a few websites for finding reliable copies of the poems in each lesson, these sites sometimes have multimedia resources associated with the poems. I also suggest further reading for teachers or additional resources and scholarship for deepening your own background knowledge on a variety of topics for study, scholarship about the teaching strategies, performance techniques, poetic techniques, academic writing, poets, and so forth.

In addition to illustrating the ways in which students can become truly engaged in critical literacy through performance and creative writing, I hope this book can serve as a useful tool in thinking more deeply about how we design lessons to promote critical literacy practices. After all, the selection of texts and tasks shapes each student's apprenticeship experience and provides the means by which we help students transform strategies into enduring skills.

In the end, I hope the 360-degree approach can help you help your students become more ardent and powerful readers and writers of all sorts of texts.

Acknowledgments

I'd like to acknowledge Margaret, my Uncle Joe, Gita, Meredyth, Ally, Tanya, Camille, and Ami, who have pulled my weight so often, in so many ways. I would also like to thank the wonderfully encouraging and smart reader, Bonny Graham at NCTE, whose concise feedback has guided this project from its vague beginning. All of these people and others are in many ways responsible for this final product, minus any big mistakes, of course; those are all mine. I am also eternally grateful to Kelley Prosser, whose editing has given me confidence. Most of all I need to thank a few of my best close reading and writing teachers, Dan Sackett, David Jolliffe, Jim Fairhall, Eric Murphy Selinger, and Gerald Graff.

I Theory and Research

1 A Research Base for the 360-Degree Approach

And gladly wolde he lerne, and gladly teche
—Geoffrey Chaucer

Why Teach Students to Describe the Meaning of Texts?

Before I explain the 360-degree approach to teaching close reading and powerful writing, I think it is important for me to explain why I think it is our job in the first place. Simply put, as English teachers we have to empower all our students to use texts to construct and represent meaning skillfully, because by every measure, it gives them a better chance at having a better life. In addition to these very practical concerns, good education is and ought to be about thinking, and successful students are engaged in thinking about texts. No matter where one stands in the spectrum of education stakeholders, everyone, from the staunchest conservatives to the most radical progressives, believes that critical literacy is one thing that ought to be nurtured. Even our most high-stakes sorting mechanisms, which sometimes seem to have taken over, reward critical literacy. College and career readiness by many definitions, including the Common Core State Standards, is in large part measured by one's ability to make meaning of complex texts and create fluent, evidence-based arguments about them (Common Core). By engaging students effectively with rich texts that challenge them to do increasingly more complex cognitive work, we help students become more skilled at getting more out of texts. We help them become more astute and autonomous sense makers and more fluent and sophisticated claim makers.

In this book I offer ideas about how students might become more skilled in constructing and representing meaning for personal and academic purposes through effective engagement with rich sample texts (in this case, poems) and fruit-bearing cognitive tasks (performance, creative writing, and traditional academic reading and writing, such as explication and debate.) The 360-degree approach to textual analysis helps teachers instill intellectual values by engaging students with big ideas about which they may already be concerned and showing them the meaningful results of that engagement through close reading and academic writing. I believe that by matching the text to the task we can show students the fruits of their intellectual labors more quickly, thereby encouraging them to continue practicing these intellectual moves on increasingly diverse and complex texts.

In developing the 360-degree approach to independent textual power, I have focused on developing procedural and metacognitive knowledge—the skills, techniques, and methods for reading challenging texts and moving beyond comprehension to critical analysis. The activities I suggest deliberately attend to the "how to understand or create text" but also one of the trickiest parts (in my experience) of teaching English, awareness of one's own thinking in response to these tasks (Anderson and Krathwohl).

I have developed this scope and sequence as a result of thinking for years about a few questions: Which skills are most valuable for constructing and representing meaning in all kinds of texts? How can I break that desirable skill or set of skills into engaging moves or strategies students can practice over and over again until they become automatic? When that strategy is employed, which text will yield fruit that kids want to eat? In other words, does this text with this task give me an opportunity to promote textual power, metacognitive awareness, and intellectual values?

We sometimes aren't successful at engaging students, no matter how hard we try. But we have to try hard if, ultimately, we want students to get excited about text and their own textual power. I hope to increase the odds of this gamble by offering an engaging and fruitful 360-degree tour.

What Is the 360-Degree Approach?

The 360-degree approach allows students to gain textual power by exploring and creating engaging, complex texts by spiraling back to their own work as meaning makers as they read/view/hear, discuss, perform, and write texts of all kinds. Exploiting heightened student engagement and the unique cognitive fruits of performance, creative writing, and argument/debate activities, the approach carefully scaffolds and supports the exploration of text from the inside out, allowing students to see how the choices of artists and academic authors contribute to meaning.

Independence is what we want our students to achieve, so autonomy is what we need to support. Along the 360-degree tour, students investigate texts through a full spectrum of learning modalities until they find a range of strategies for approaching texts that work well for them. In addition to a variety of learning strategies, I advocate a variety of autonomy-supportive instructional modes: "I do it" to "we do it together" to "you do it together" and, finally, to "you do it alone" (Ivey and Fisher 13).

Strategies, from performance games to templates for thinking aloud to peer workshops, help students practice and understand the cognitive

[margin handwritten note, left:] A Taxonomy for Learning, Teaching, and Assessing: A Revision of Bloom's Taxonomy of Educational Objectives

[margin handwritten note, left:] Support Autonomy

[margin handwritten note, left:] Creating Literacy-Rich Schools for Adolescents

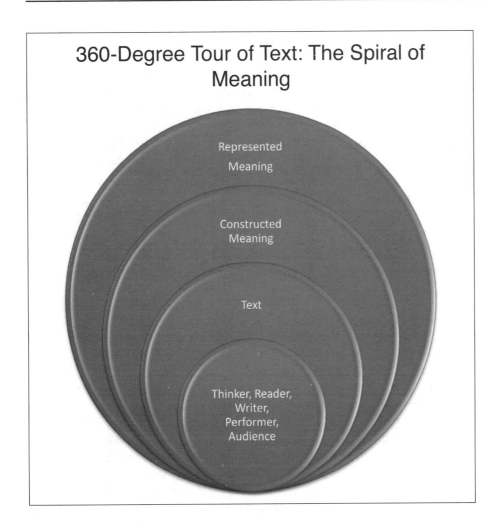

processes involved in constructing and representing meaning. These strategies ultimately work to take some of the mystery out of analytical reading, thinking, and writing, allowing teachers to gradually release responsibility for textual analysis and claim making to their students.

My ultimate hope is that eventually when your students ask, "How did you get that?" they will be challenging your interpretation, not wondering about the mysterious functions of the English teacher's mind.

How Templates Support Autonomy

To some, templates and autonomy may sound like contradictory terms. But the templates I advocate in the 360-degree approach support autonomy by scaffolding and supporting the processes (as well as some of the verbal fluency) involved in constructing and representing textual meaning to others. In order for students to develop a procedural knowledge of how to gather meaning from texts, they need a vocabulary for describing the metacognitive processes that lead to meaning. Furthermore, making evidence-based claims about text requires a special kind of academic fluency that becomes more comfortable with experience.

This template approach works like training wheels. Instead of simultaneously learning all the moves involved in riding a bike, training wheels allow a rider to overcome a fear of falling long enough to enjoy the pleasures of moving forward faster and faster and steering the bike in the direction the rider wants to go. Like training wheels, the templates help students concentrate on automatizing certain meaning-making moves. Each template scaffolds toward the ultimate act of independence, constructing and representing meaning in the mode of their choice and articulating it with confidence to another reader.

Today, unlike our kindergarten selves who concentrated all our efforts on decoding letter sounds, we make meaning of all sorts of texts all day long, without even realizing we are reading text. The step-by-step process that led you from decoder to comprehender to analyst isn't as simple to chart as the steps in acquiring phonemic awareness, yet today when you read a literary text, you visualize to comprehend, make personal connections with the text, connect the text to other texts, and connect the text to the world, often without thinking about it. Frequently, as an experienced reader and analyst, you are unlikely to think much about *how* you were able to make these connections, unless you are challenged by another reader or are reading a more challenging text, in which case you stop yourself and reflect on the text and your thinking until you have validated the evidence to support a certain meaning. Your teachers, your literary apprenticeship, and many years of reading led you to this point. Providing explicit experiences like these is what we must do for our students, since so often young readers don't just pick it up on their own.

This tour provides a sort of charted path for your students, as spiraling as it may be, to help students understand explicitly how to make the smart moves that are often intimidating to novice readers.

Some of our students may still be struggling to decode the meaning of new words or to visualize, and most of our students have not yet reached a level of automaticity in connecting with texts on a variety of levels to make interpretive claims about literary texts. These templates offer students a support that helps them break these processes into smaller steps until each step becomes more or less automatic.

How Templates Scaffold toward Academic Writing

Far from being restrictive, the templates, when used well, can work like idea machines that help students generate thoughts about texts. These templates came from one of the practical realities of teaching English: the teacher's inability to sit with every student long enough, prompting them to explain: "What makes you think that? Why? Tell me more, tell me more."

Think-Aloud Prompts (handouts 1.C and 5.B in the appendix) raise student awareness of how master readers respond to and interact with textual choices, making explicit the process by which readers take text *in* and make meaning. What comes *out* during think-aloud is what happened in the reader's brain, something that sounds like, "This makes me picture . . ." This metacognitive practice supports automaticity by giving students, including English language learners (ELLs), many informal opportunities to talk descriptively and analytically with others about the effect of certain elements of texts and to hash out meaning before being asked to write formally. These templates also reinforce the values of inquiry and evidence that are the heart and soul of academic argument.

In the imitative writing stage, additional Think-Aloud Prompts help students notice more advanced features of the text, such as form and technique, as well as pattern and variation, awareness of which are essential to making larger claims about text. In conjunction with the Key Terms handouts (1.B and 5.A in the appendix), students begin to develop the habits and vocabulary they need to describe texts for formal academic purposes.

In the workshop phase, students take the next step, making descriptive claims about peer-authored works. Using the Workshop Templates (handout 5.E in the appendix), students learn to make claim statements that state the effect of authorial choices. The language of the template is still familiar and informal, but the template itself reflects the constituent parts of formal claims. Students practice speaking of text in terms of authors making choices. In this case, they are using peer authors as live sounding boards. "When you did X, it made me picture X, because when most people think of X, they think X. When you said X, I thought you meant X," and so on.

The final set of templates helps students analyze text for academic writing and compose formal academic claims. The Describing Text Templates (handout 9.E in the appendix) help students formalize the language they use to make claims, prompting them to articulate explicitly, formally, and more elegantly the reasoning behind their claims. Similar to the underlying format of the claims used in the Workshop Templates, the students' sentences focus on their interpretation of an author's choice. To put it simply, students deepen and formalize their thinking about texts powerfully on paper: "The image suggests X."

The Describing Text Templates also help students prepare to write formal explications by facilitating more critical interactions with samples of the kind of writing we ask them to produce. Having students use the templates as a lens through which they can understand academic writing helps them approach some of the intimidating features of such writing with less anxiety and helps them master the language of the pros more readily. Obviously, repeated practice in describing texts in the language of the pros prepares students to read professional scholarship, while reading professional scholarship, in turn, prepares students to write it more adeptly.

Why Use Poetry to Help Students Develop Textual Power?

In short: poetry is rich, ornate, and compact. But that's not all.[1]

Unfortunately, students have had bad experiences with poetry. Many teachers themselves have had bad experiences with poetry as students. As a result, some say, they avoid poetry, confessing that they don't feel comfortable dealing with poetry. I've never heard any English teacher say such things about novels or any other whole genre, but poetry has often been written about and talked about in ways that make it seem difficult.

I believe poetry is one of the most nourishing ways to nurture the omnivorous young reader. To that end, I have tried to spell out simple, pleasurable ways of approaching poetry while helping students develop skills they can use in any genre.

After all, the signs that students respond well to poetry are all around us. Youth culture, from lyrics scribbled on notebook covers and poems "spit" from the stages of poetry slams, gives ample evidence that adolescents find poetry inspiring and intellectually engaging, perhaps even necessary in their own self-exploration and self-expression. They really are ready to appreciate the beauty of its formal elements and, in my experience, are often delighted when they are challenged to do so.

What Makes Performance an Effective Approach to Teaching Close Reading?

Performance can be a route to genuine engagement and rigor. And to those experiences, every student has a right. Research shows that an oral interpretation approach to literary texts increases comprehension, reading rates, and literary appreciation. Done frequently enough and well enough, I believe, poetry performance assignments can help increase the overall academic achievement and cultural literacy of the reader/performer and his or her audience. Jeffrey Wilhelm, a leading researcher in the area, argues that because it is action-oriented and participatory, performance-based strategies "begin with and are driven by student interests, by what they already know and find significant and by what is socially relevant" (*Action Strategies* 11). As Wilhelm notes, whether it is a group performance or a recitation, the intrinsic social quality of performance capitalizes on Vygotsky's idea that all learning is social.

The unique level of engagement in text that performance requires often motivates students to practice the habits of expert readers, effective reading strategies that transfer across the curriculum. "Performing a poem, using the whole body with limbs, facial expression, and voice, requires students to go farther in understanding a poem than does strip-mining poems for technical terms" (Ellis, Ruggles Gere, and Lamberton 46). As they rehearse, students use repeated rereading for comprehension, recall prior knowledge to make personal connections to the text, monitor and test assumptions, and sometimes entertain conflicting interpretations of text. "Dramatic expression is evidence of the internal construction of literary meaning and the reader's perception of the act of the reading" (Ortleib, Cramer, and Cheek). Repeated practice with these strategies promotes increased confidence in meaning making and a heightened awareness of author's craft.

"Oral interpretation can serve as a site for thinking about what meanings writers communicate, as well as how interpreters become communicators" (Banks 51). Students begin to connect texts to their personal experiences as they think about how to use their own bodies and voices to make the experience of the speaker visible to others. First, students are genuinely constructing meaning. They are figuring out what the speaker of a poem is saying. Then, they have to perform the closest of readings to determine how the text cues them to represent this meaning by visualizing facial expressions and gestures, as well as imagining the voices of the speakers they will embody.

In *"You Gotta BE the Book,"* Wilhelm cites research that indicates that the "the ability to use imagery is a central difference between good and poor readers" (118). The visualization strategies we teach to poor readers and assume are part of the good readers' repertoire are authentically prompted by performance. Additionally, students are thinking about how the meaning of this speaker's words should shape their tone of voice, facial expressions, volume, and body language, among other things, in performance. Simply put, when students are charged with communicating interpretation, they are motivated to explore and communicate the meaning of text in much deeper, more imaginative ways. This kind of practice at the meaning level of a poem is one of the richest experiences in critical literacy we can provide for our students. More importantly, these activities can be a source of absolute delight, which is truly valuable in promoting academic success for all students.

Just like actors, as students attempt to embody the speaker in a poem, they are motivated to perform authentic rereadings, monitoring and testing their own process of meaning making. "Repeated readings become rehearsals, and those rehearsals before their peers and an eventual performance provide the incentive to practice reading the same passage repeatedly" (Goodson and Goodson 26). Goodson and Goodson's work shows increased test scores among participating students, suggesting that increased levels of engagement with the text, resulting from performance activities, motivated students to find pleasure in literature, read more, and read faster and better than before.

The challenge of preparing for performance results in more serious attention to author's craft as well. Students explore the "elasticity of the words, to appreciate how different readings of the same lines can be supported by the text," as English teacher and NCTE author John S. O'Connor notes (99). He adds, "It is more difficult to discern subtext when reading than when seeing an actor perform, since the actor's facial expressions, gestures, and vocal inflections help draw subtextual material to the surface." For the performer, the process of constructing a performance requires a close examination of subtext and provides genuine motivation for entertaining conflicting interpretations of text (Goodson and Goodson 29). More than an academic essay or even a classroom discussion, performance for an audience or ensemble of peers authentically compels students to hash out various interpretations of texts as they make performance choices. Inviting students to have those debates through performance is a wonderful way to engage students meaningfully in the same cognitive work performed in evidence-based argumentation, the very basis of scholarship across the curriculum.

Performance strategies for teaching poetry can help English teachers do what they do best: everything at once. As English teacher and author Judy Rowe Michaels notes,

> When we move on [after performances] to writing a more traditional and analytical essay on a shorter contemporary poem, students have gained confidence in their ability to respond to a poem

personally, with their senses and imagination, to relate individual moments to the whole, to read closely but accept some ambiguities—in short, to make meaning. (53–54)

In addition to becoming authentic meaning-making readers, students have the opportunity, through recitation and other performances, to garner new language—beautiful, meaningful, and empowering language. After all, a great command of language is necessary in the same sense that college has become necessary. In the twenty-first century, everyone must engage in demanding and consequential communication activities within and without the walls of academia. To a certain extent, close reading, close listening, close viewing, and the deliberate articulation of complex ideas in complex situations are basic survival skills today. We need to deepen, expand, and increase the sophistication of our students' personal linguistic resources.

We teachers are responsible for giving our students the most important key to success in their adult lives: the key to literacy in their collegiate, professional, and personal lives. Whether communicating via technology or speaking in public, our students need guided practice in these skills. What better, more pleasurable way than literature out loud? In sharing the pleasures of poems, we give students meaningful experiences with artful language, self-expression, emotional and intellectual insight, and perhaps even the empathy and reassurance poetry can offer in navigating their complex lives. Performances are substantive ways to address reading, writing, listening, and speaking standards that were written in recognition of these facts.

Perhaps the most compelling piece of research I have to offer in favor of a particular kind of performance, recitation, is based on the work of a historian at the University of Rochester. In her book *Songs of Ourselves: The Uses of Poetry in America,* Joan Shelley Rubin includes a study of the legacy of poetry recitation assignments. Her data were the nearly five hundred letters she received in response to a query in the *New York Review of Books*. Her research examined the lasting effects of poetry recitation assignments in schools between 1917 and 1950.

Letters reflected the innumerable and surprising effects of this once commonly assigned school activity. Nearly all of the respondents shared positive stories of how the assignment enriched their lives. Notably, those who shared negative experiences attributed their distaste to the way in which the assignment was presented by their teacher, rather than the assignment itself.

Recitation assignments were common at the time for many reasons. In addition to the academic benefits of practicing memorization or public speaking, students were encouraged to recite as a means of acquiring appreciation of other technical elements. "Several respondents also testified that they attained the aesthetic benefits that teachers ascribed to the recitation, explicitly mentioning rhythm, sound, and imagery as a source of delight" (Rubin 149).

While I am the greatest advocate of introducing students to the pleasures of these aesthetics, what was more interesting to me was the overwhelming number of respondents who cited the more practical application of poetry in their lives. One woman said "Invictus" helped her "hold her head up when her father, 'a Jew in KKK land,' went to prison for a crime he did not commit" (Rubin 147). Others talked about the identification they felt with poets. One man wrote that he did not feel "alone or unique in my feelings . . . not a bad thing for a twelve year old boy to know" (148). According to these testimonies, the relief of these memorized poems was called upon from operating tables, boardrooms, desolate mining camps, and battlefields.

Some respondents also reported the electrifying effect the assignment and particular texts had upon whole families. One woman recalled her astonishment as a fourth grader struggling to memorize a poem, when her father "began saying the poem. And said it to the end. With feeling. That glimpse of continuity and linkage between my father and me has stayed with me these fifty-six years" (Rubin 153).

These incredible stories remind me of the great responsibility and privilege we have as English teachers. The voices of this research are the voices of our students speaking to us from the future, reminding us how important every minute and every text are, test or no test. As we strive to improve our students' chances of being successful in academia, we also have to remember why poetry and other forms of literature merited a place in academia in the first place. It matters universally. Poetry as an art form is common to every civilization because it matters to all human beings.

What Is the Best Way to Get Students Started with Performance?

I'm neither an actor nor a director; I am an English teacher. Yet, I have found myself modeling performance and asking students to perform ever since I began teaching. I have been lucky enough to attend a number of wonderful workshops presented by Chicago theaters and, through them and scholars such as Jeffrey Wilhelm, have learned that the best way to get started with performance is simply to get everyone performing and to think of performing as playing. If everyone can commit to having fun and taking risks the way they would in a playground game, students and teachers can do amazing things in just a few minutes in any ad hoc performance space.

The Performance Plans

The sequence of poems in Chapter 2 comes with a step-by-step guide to introducing close reading strategies and performance methods that help students both construct and represent meaning. It helps students practice the fundamental moves of close reading by reading to prepare an embodiment of the imagined speaker. In addition to guidance on the close reading strategies students will need to prepare performances, I have built in a number of very simple trust-building and improvisation activities to equip students with tools that can be used to create both ad hoc and fully staged performances.

Starting with what students already know, their personal stories, students build a supportive environment by listening to each other and risking a moment of public sharing. After reading each of several poems, students have the opportunity to practice with key improvisational tools: silent sculpture, tableau, role-playing, and slide show. With these four tools alone, students have everything they need to begin staging great group performances of even the most complex texts. Recitation activities throughout the rest of the book build on the trust and knowledge of earlier group performances but place the onus of communicating meaning on the individual performer. The sections that follow provide my best general advice on using performance in the English classroom, gathered through nearly two decades of trial and error, along with a list of trusted resources on the subject.

Performance Space

If we want our students to play, we need a playground. If you are lucky enough to have an actual alternative space, great. If not, you just need to move the desks or go out into a hallway or a field. Any open space can be a performance space. For many initial activities, a circle within that open space works just fine. For more formal performances, you may want to set up a more formal space for an audience.

Warm-up

We all carry ourselves in certain ways that help us feel more confident or at least less vulnerable. Day to day, we practice keeping our distance from each other, crossing our legs, folding our arms around a book, or averting our eyes. This physical armor has to go when we commit to playing. Physical theater games, even the hokey pokey, free the voice and the body from the defensive, nonperformer stance in which most of us live, and having fun together makes students feel safer about taking the risk of performing. Videos of all kinds of theater games are available online, but for quick reference, here are five of my favorite icebreakers:

- Give students one minute to *silently* group themselves by shoe type, then by height, then other categories (e.g., shoe color, shirt type, etc.).
- Have students sit with a partner and share a one-minute story about a gift they really, really wanted as a kid but never got or got and loved.
- Have pairs of students mime each other trying on clothes or washing a window.
- Have students silently stare at each other in the eyes for a full sixty seconds. Keep doing it until the whole class is successful. This is hard, but it goes a long way to breaking down our invisible barriers.
- Have each student enter a circle made by classmates sitting cross-legged on the floor and share a one-minute story of an emotionally intense moment (accompanied by a single, emblematic gesture). After five beats they leave the circle. (See Chapter 2, lesson 1 for further explanation of this technique.)

Ensemble Play

Give the performers time to play with a script as an ensemble. Encouraging play among equals, rather than assigning a director, gets students to engage in interpretation, perhaps even evidence-based argumentation about literary texts. Don't preempt it by giving the interpretive power over to one student director.

Physical Vocabulary

Physical vocabulary is a physical image or motion that represents an idea. For example, a fist is anger, pointing a finger is accusation, praying hands is reverence. Have students develop a physical vocabulary: a group or class agrees upon a few overarching themes or images from a text, creates a physical representation of each key idea, and, from the physical representations, weaves together an ensemble performance by representing the key ideas or themes physically. "Still I Rise" is a poem that plays upon the image of rising up against forces that would keep the speaker down, so the physical vocabulary—that is, the positions and gestures of the ensemble members—might show highs and lows, rising and falling, force and resistance. Zeroing in on a key image is a great way for students to begin thinking about the coherency of various elements of a work centered on a particular theme. Later on, when you begin talking about claims, you might refer back to earlier physical vocabulary activities, reminding students that just as they were able to identify a major unifying image in performance, they will be learning to describe these unifying themes and images in writing.

In addition to practicing image analysis, students will also be more capable of recognizing and describing the impact of authorial choices when they see the impact of choice in performance. For example, the tempo of a performer's entrance to a stage has meaning, as does the tempo of a spoken line of text; the image of an actor in relation to a setting has meaning, as does the image conjured by words on a page. Connecting parts to the whole is the key.

Guidelines

Guidelines help students play better by challenging them to use a wider range of performance tools than they might have chosen on their own. Here are a few examples of guidelines I use, sometimes one or several at a time, sometimes all at once:

- Use individual, dual, and choral voices at least once each during the performance.
- Use the entire performance space (all four "corners" of the "stage" area).
- Use all levels of the performance space (sitting/lying down, kneeling, and standing levels).
- Start or end with a tableau (an arrangement of performers' bodies that is like a painting).
- Use at least one or two images of physical vocabulary to underscore a theme.
- Silently move the focus—the viewer's attention—from one performer to another with a recurring cue such as a bow, freezing motion, or a quick turning away or repeated emblematic action, such as a gesture that has thematic significance. The focus technique indicates a performer has been turned off and another is on.

Celebrating Performance

Whether students are performing original or published poems, as a group or as individuals, attention must be paid. Making a special occasion of a performance is not very difficult. A simple change in lighting, time, or location can make a performance more special. After all, if students have really invested in a performance, they ought to get a stage, an audience, and perhaps some refreshments or awards when possible. Any one or all of these variations from the day-to-day routine will help students celebrate textual power and share their enthusiasm with others.

As you and your students organize your production, remember that performing poems through recitation or dramatization is doubly good. For every valuable moment students spend on the preparation of performances, from selecting the poem to preparing an interpretation, they are engaged in critical reading. In the most engaged stance a reader can take, students then become the speakers of the poems, offering an accessible presentation of a text for their audience. Rather than simply waiting for their turn to speak, you will see students engage with the performance, so the classroom audience walks away with an effortless, often wonderful, experience of literature. I can't think of a more fun and exciting way to develop cultural literacy, to invite students to make connections to texts and between other texts and their worlds.

Transforming a Performance Space into a Writer's Studio

One of the added benefits of playing with performance is that it lays all the important foundations for the creative writing leg of the 360-degree tour. Whether students are practicing to be more astute readers, better performers, poets, or more artful academic writers, the playground for performance is a nurturing place where smart people are engaged in the exchange of important ideas. This sets a wonderful stage for a writer's workshop as well.

What Is Think-Aloud, and Why Does It Work?

Supporting the development of critical reading skills and fluency in the language of textual analysis along the way, each lesson in Chapter 2 provides opportunities for teachers to model and encourage our tribal talk through the use of think-alouds and key literary terms. "Think-alouds are a reader's verbalization in reaction to reading a selection" (Caldwell 191). First developed by a product usability expert at IBM, think-alouds help students make visible to others their responses to text and the "normally covert mental processes" they use to comprehend text (as quoted in Caldwell 191). The tool allows teachers to assess readers while simultaneously offering instruction in independent approaches to text. In large and small groups, this approach to discussion creates rich collaborative opportunities for students who read and write about literature together.

As part of the social and participatory "out loud" approach to poetry that I advocate, think-aloud helps students develop the meta-cognitive habits of expert readers. Visualization and other interpretive skills essential to poetry reading are not always automatic, as expert readers sometimes assume. In some cases, students need instruction to develop this automaticity. "Teachers need to explain how to think to their students; that is, we need to model, describe, explain, and scaffold appropriate reading strategies" (Afflerbach, Pearson, and Paris). Think-aloud, an independence-promoting alternative to traditional, predetermined discussion questions, illuminates the impact of approaching texts with deliberate strategies. "Now imagine that the strategy works and the student continues to use it throughout the school year. With months of practice, the strategy requires less deliberate attention, and the student uses it more quickly and more efficiently. When it becomes effortless and automatic (i.e., the student is in the habit of asking 'Does that make sense?' automatically), the reading strategy has become a reading skill" (Afflerbach, Pearson, and Paris). The goal of think-aloud and of all the lessons in this book is to help students interact with texts independently and feel confident that they have the skill to make meaning of poetry, or any other kind of text, no matter how complex. Without the confidence and know-how that these prompts stimulate, students can't legitimately be expected to write and support formal academic claims about text.

Structured and monitored oral practice with academic discourse using this common vocabulary is empowering for students, especially for ELLs. One by one, through the use of Think-Aloud Prompts and Key Literary Terms, students discover that the words expert readers use are actually gateways to comprehension, not just fancy descriptors designed to keep others at a distance. As students practice the cognitive processes of generating more sophisticated statements about texts, they have richer conversations with peers and become more capable participants in the intellectual communities they enter.

Think-aloud also enhances particular aspects of creative and academic writing instruction. *English Journal* contributor and English teacher Nelson Graff advocates using think-aloud on published texts as practice for peer workshops. These think-aloud–oriented workshops then focus on helping young authors understand the impact of their choices. Graff argues, "If students are to respond to each other's drafts as they would to published texts, they need practice responding to published texts as they would each other's drafts" (81). "[When] students practice thinking aloud with published texts before they do so with each other's texts, they build the habit of thinking aloud to understand rather than to 'fix'; and, because students return during peer review to explicit reading strategies, they become more strategic readers" (81). Through repeated teacher modeling and the use of think-aloud sentence starters that prompt the deliberate use of these cognitive moves, students become fluent in the moves and the language of analyzing text, the tricks of the trade that have made literature teachers the successful readers they are.

In the practical chapters, I have provided models of thinking aloud that I have used to make my thought process visible to my students. These are not teacher scripts, but examples to show the ways in which we can scaffold the reading and interpretation of poetry for students through modeling. The prompts that are provided in the second chapter focus on developing habits such as visualizing, monitoring comprehension, summarizing, and considering the rhetorical scenario of a poem. They also help students begin considering some elements of author's craft. The second set of think-aloud prompts focuses more heavily on author's craft, particularly as it relates to form and technique. The Workshop Templates then capitalize on the habits of thinking and speaking about text that the Think-Aloud Prompts encouraged, while laying the foundation for more formal claims in explications. The template builds upon Think-Aloud Prompts such as "This makes me picture . . . " by placing it into the context of describing the effect of a peer author's choice. The Describing Text Templates take it one step further, prompting students to talk about author choices more formally.

Does Creative Writing Really Make Our Students Better Academic Readers and Writers?

As the Mathematics Department chair mounted yet another plaque for our school's award-winning math team, he gibed that the department I chaired had fairly bare walls in comparison. Though our students had won many accolades in creative writing and performance, I feebly defended, "Most of our contests don't award plaques." He quipped, "Hmm. You'd think people in your field would know something about PR." Aside from the fact that the moment felt like a small defeat in our friendly interdepartmental competition, the comment also struck me because he was right. The creative writing people did have a PR problem. And I am ashamed to say it was bigger than he thought.

Even if we were to have more shiny plaques, we creative writing types would still have trouble convincing others, even colleagues in our own department, that these were signs of success for our discipline. In the English departments of several schools where I have taught, and often in the national English education conversation, these achievements are not recognized as *academic* achievements. Interestingly, in *Textual Power,* Robert Scholes comments on the terms *art* and *artist* as well as the missing counterpart of *literature* and *literaturist.* He contends, "The prestige of literature is so great that we have a taboo against naming the one who creates it. In our culture literature has been positioned in much the same place as scripture" (12). If this is indeed the case, perhaps the idea of a mere student creating something worthy of being called literature is just too ludicrous to be taken seriously. How difficult it must have been for poor Keats.

To be sure, everyone duly acknowledges creative writing's importance in offering students opportunities for self-expression; I need not argue for that here. However, instruction of that sort is rarely touted as a strategy for traditional academic success. At some extremes, it is even perceived as a break from real work, a frivolous unit for feel-good purposes. In fact, for every teacher I know who uses it enthusiastically, it seems I have met five more whose attitudes toward creative writing approaches to literary education and writing instruction range from condescension to downright loathing or horror.

Incriminatingly, teachers are not required to learn strategies for teaching creative writing as they are required to learn the pedagogy of composition or reading comprehension, and creative writing is never tested. While this *not required, not tested* condition is a blessing in many ways, it also indicates that creative writing instruction does not have a real academic status, leaving us with less research and less discussion about how to do it and why. As Christian Knoeller points out, "researchers such as James Moffett and James Britton have repeatedly suggested, [school-sponsored writing] has too often gravitated toward an unnecessarily narrow subset of the many possible purposes, audiences, and, importantly, textual types" (43). Knoeller argues "against the double-standard prevalent in our schools that assigns reading fiction and poetry as 'literature,' yet requires students to write primarily exposition" (43). Prompted by my students' success and the compelling arguments researchers like these make for the use of creative writing in every English classroom, I share these lessons to give practical examples of how this type of instruction can provide unique supports, not only for young authors but also for the equally important academic purpose of increasing the skill of literature and composition students.

I encourage the use of imitation as a springboard for creative and analytical writing instruction throughout the 360-degree approach. Imitation is useful as a tool for understanding the effect of techniques or meaning, or as Helen Vendler puts it, the relation between matter and manner

(114). It is also a route to understanding the language of literature, which can make literary scholarship, the kind that students are often asked to read and produce, appear impenetrable. Finally, it offers a valuable assessment tool that might appeal to students in ways that traditional academic writing does not. In *English Journal*, Alfie Kohn recently suggested that one sure way to kill student motivation is by limiting choice in terms of how their understanding is assessed (18). If he's right, excluding imaginative writing from the range of valid assessment choices is a shame.

I close my case on this point with an important but rarely argued point for creative writing in every English classroom. Researcher, professor, and former high school English teacher Christian Knoeller asserts that imaginative responses are also an effective alternative to academic writing for assessing literary understanding. Like others of us who have used these strategies, he argues that creative writing assignments have academic value beyond helping students understand literary technique or engaging training modules for analytical prose imitation assignments. When students create original imaginative works in response to literature, they sometimes become engaged in better reading and connect more authentically with their writing about literature. He argues, "allowing students to express original responses in a wide variety of genres ultimately gives more of them, not only those adept at analytic prose, a personally meaningful way to engage with literature" (43). The large body of work by researchers such as Jeffrey Wilhelm provides indisputable evidence that creative writing, like performance, can be used as a learning and assessment tool to increase achievement in English. As Knoeller so eloquently puts it, "rather than supplanting conventional literary criticism in the classroom, such writing—what I term imaginative response—can readily complement and ultimately enrich formal analysis" (42). Responding imaginatively to a literary text often motivates students with an authentic need to do the work of reading for meaning and to construct more deliberately their own thoughtful texts for both academic and artistic purposes. Commenting on the work of educational reformer Mike Schmoker in his 2008 "Research Matters" column, Rick VanDeWeghe says, "close reading is not mysterious, not something that only certain kinds of advanced readers can do. Rather, 'such reading starts with good questions and prompts' . . . , and such reading is done for meaning" (106). Imaginative responses engage students with text in ways other assignments cannot, raising good questions that are not always brought out by traditional written assessments.

The long-standing pedagogical tradition of imitation is based on the idea of paying attention to detail, from the overall structure of a text, right down to the level of word choice. Simply put, advocates for the imitative approach, even ancient ones, believe that the more exposure students have to good models (both imaginative and academic), the more freedom of choice they have in their own work. In his article "The Art of Imitation," *English Journal* contributor J. Scott Shields cites the work of researcher James Murphy, who finds that Roman rhetorical pedagogy provided students with instruction through imitation, equipping them with the freedom to select and strategically deploy the tools of great writers, poets, and politicians alike (Shields).

Like performance, imitative writing demands that students explore a text closely to see technique at work in the creation of meaning. One *Voices from the Middle* contributor likens the act of reading for imitative purposes to mining for gems. In her article about using journals to record favorite words and phrases, Pat Thomas sees her middle school students "searching for those [gems], which will help create the ideal text they have in mind" (235). Guided practice in this mining work and experience in deploying the tools they discover deepens our students' reserve of linguistic resources and challenges students to develop a command over these tools. With this textual power, students can engage in more deliberate choice making in their own writing for all occasions.

Whether your goal is to empower writers with tools or to help students really appreciate the art of literary texts, as Robert Scholes argues in *The Crafty Reader*, or even to help students read with an expert kind of appreciation, as Robert Pinsky suggests, connecting an accessible model with sophisticated imitative reading and writing prompts is good pedagogy. In *With Rigor for All*, past NCTE president Carol Jago supports such pedagogy, stating that teachers "need to take the time in class to show students how to examine a text in minute detail: word by word, sentence by sentence" (54). "Only then," Jago asserts, "will [students] develop the skills they need to be powerful readers" (55). Both modeling close reading in this way and asking students to mine these models for material and forms they might use in their own original writing are essential steps in empowering our students with the levels of literacy that higher education and the twenty-first century demand.

In terms of the academic value of this sort of practice, those of us who have regularly used it know that imitating imaginative works is a wonderful stepping-stone to imitation in analytical prose. The processes, routines, and strategies for close reading that students establish in creative writing workshops can transform their approach to writing traditional academic texts as well. In fact, I would argue that these two ventures—teaching students to write poems and teaching students to write essays—are part of the same enterprise. After all, tempering a sentence for either poetic or argumentative effect requires engaging with the same set of skills.

Actively exploring the effect of a particular technique from the vantage point of a writer also enhances a student's ability to understand and respond to the often jargonistic analytical prose found in poetry scholarship, as well as other disciplines in the humanities. As in learning to write a poem, the step in critical discourse that comes after saying something meaningful is revising, bringing the most effective and precise language to bear in service of meaning. The value of understanding form, genre, and other technical aspects of literature and being able to use the language in precise and sophisticated ways cannot be overstated in relation to its impact on understanding scholarship about the texts.

Finally, and it should go without saying, don't we owe it to the next Shakespeare, Dante, García Márquez, or Morrison, who may be sitting in front of us today, to teach creative writing, just as we owe it to the next Einstein to teach math?

How Can We Facilitate Writers Workshops with Artistic and Academic Benefits?

Many of us would agree that great literature helps us explore enduring questions about being human. For all of us, but especially adolescents who may be exploring some of these questions for the first time, this is powerful stuff, and when we engage with it deeply, our responses tend to be powerful also. Anyone who has taught adolescents knows that an invitation to share ideas about important issues can also be an opportunity for students to share difficult experiences or uncomfortable points of view. Therefore, writers workshops require safe places and appropriate models of how to respond to each other both as learners and evolving human beings.

The first step in facilitating a writers workshop is creating a contract with students defining the ethics and obligations involved in being members of such a creative writing community. The imitative exercises and the suggested creative writing activities that follow each lesson in Chapter 2 invite students to explore and respond to issues of identity, struggle, memory, triumph, family, and other experiences that prompt students to engage with text in powerful ways. Teachers who take on this (legal and ethical) responsibility develop some of the richest relationships teachers and students can share. Below are the two most important pieces of advice I can give to creating this nurturing place:

- *Change the physical setting or set-up.* If possible, change the location or at least the arrangement of students. I am a fan of the circle, as the ideal of equality is important to me. Also, in my teaching I have found that the room setup has to allow swift transitions from individual work to small groups to large groups. Perhaps that is one reason why I also like to move to the floor for workshops. Fun drills can help train your students to arrange the desks quickly, and the floor somehow moves the whole enterprise of learning together into another realm for students, making it more a part of our real lives than other desk-based activities. Students sometimes reject this, and in some cases it is more than a miniskirt that makes it downright impossible for a student to sit on the floor. I respect these individual situations and make appropriate adjustments.

- *Engage and celebrate every student's contribution.* Everyone must participate in every step, though not every single time. Be very conscious that every student shares multiple experiences of drafting, gathering feedback, and providing feedback. Don't let the quiet ones, the shy ones, and the ones that say they "hate writing" miss out on the knowledge they can construct only by articulating their ideas in the workshop. I discuss this further when I talk about revision.

Honoring the Drafting Process with Class Time

An important step in facilitating writers workshop is honoring student writing (creative and academic) with class time for initial drafting. This might seem like a no-brainer to some, but given the everything-at-once responsibility of teaching English, time limitations do force us to make some tough choices. Many teachers feel that initial drafting is something that students can do on their own. One may even argue, as students often do, that home is the best place to get initial ideas onto paper. I advocate spending some time on initial drafting in class by giving students what I call Sacred Silent Writing Time (SSWT). This is one way I show my students that no assignment I give is the kind one might scribble on the bus, just so I have something to record in my grade book when I am bored at home. If it is worth doing at all, I tell them, it is important enough for us to do in class, free from distraction.

When the process is new to students, this is also the time to clarify procedural questions, allay fears in person, and set the stage for treating the physical space of the classroom as a working writer's studio. Here are three more words to the wise:

- *Protect SSWT at all costs.* Don't let anything disrupt it. Especially at the beginning, it is essential to protect this like a hawk until the routine is set and respect for that time is gained. Change the lighting. Allow students to write wherever they want, even if that means lying on the floor. Do whatever it takes to demarcate this time from other classroom activities.

- *Don't accept no for an answer, and don't over-explain.* Every student has to write something—even if it is a grocery list. I'm not kidding. Have a student with a blank page write a grocery list, then rewrite the same list for an alien who will do the shopping. (What a great lesson on the impact of audience on writing choices!) Whatever you do, just don't let any student leave with a blank page. Circulate, and don't let them burn up their SSWT with what-do-*you*-want questions. This is a student's piece; try not to fall into the trap of explaining your ideal text. Write good prompts and stick to them; then allow students to spring from prompts to writing what they feel they need to write. You need only create the demand for self-expression.

- *Once SSWT is established, write with your fellow writers.* Setting up the routines and expectations of this time takes a great deal of circulation at first. After the routine gets rolling, though, use the time to write. But don't write emails, lesson plans, or comments on student papers; as often as possible, write your own responses to the prompts. Remember, as the cliché goes, you are unique, just like everyone else. Your work is valued by your students not only because it is intriguing to hear about the adults in their lives, and not only because they are honored by your willingness to collapse the teacher-student hierarchy in that way, but also because they get to see that even a more experienced, more authoritative writer can use the prompts to write things worth writing.

Workshop Routines for Artistic and Academic Writing

First, let there be praise.

A whatever-you-do-is-wonderful approach to creative writing undermines a student's confidence as much as harsh criticism does, because students are smart. Empty praise for their writing leaves even the most confident students with a sneaking suspicion that their work has a face only their supportive English teacher could love. In initial drafts, journals, and other beginning places, uninhibited freedom and self-satisfaction is indispensable. But for the purposes of helping our students become better readers and writers, revision and public scrutiny by real readers is essential. So at some point, the timely, specific, and substantive praise must be accompanied by suggestions for improvement. Aside from being a great motivator, genuine praise lets students know what they are doing well, so they continue to get better at recognizing good writing when they see it and consciously making these good writerly moves.

Part of our work as writers workshop facilitators is modeling the feedback process in the same way we model discussions about professional works, using the precise and sophisticated language taught through

Key Terms and Think-Aloud Prompts. Additionally, modeling feedback is one of the most powerful ways in which creative writing instruction becomes a means of improving academic writing. A Think-Aloud Prompt such as, "This makes me picture . . . " becomes part of a Workshop Template sentence like "When you said X, it made me picture X, because when most people think of X, they think of X, because . . ." The Workshop Templates describe the effect of a writer's choice, and this is exactly the kind of interpretive sentence students will learn to write when they begin formal explications where the sentence begins to sound like "The image suggests . . ."

Now, about the resistance to creative writing revision, which comes naturally to writers, no matter their age. To that I say, workshop it. Hearts and souls are sometimes poured out in first drafts. And if this is the first time students have experimented with poetic devices or have used templates to help generate some pretty poetic-sounding text, it can be hard for them (as for all of us) to, as Faulkner puts it, kill their darlings. After all, what may seem cliché to us may not seem so to the first-time user. Despite these other quite legitimate reasons for resistance, students supported by a culture of smart, critical friends will listen to well-trained peers speaking articulately about what can and might be revised. I have found that this is the best way to sell the idea that revision can make a good piece of writing better. Indeed, I always appreciated my wonderful poetry teacher who often summed up a common thread of feedback with his tenderly ironic, signature comment: "well . . . we're all pretty smart here and we don't get it, so you might want to tinker with it."

Workshops for All

Every significant writing assignment deserves a small group writers workshop, and every student deserves a whole-class writing workshop at least once. Here are the guidelines I use when facilitating workshops in my classroom:

- *Students must use the Workshop Templates.* The templates—handout 5.E in the appendix—help students to make precise and sophisticated comments about each other's work so that students very deliberately support and nurture each other with both praise and critical feedback. Require a specific number (one to three statements) of each kind. Finally, have students write their comments, legibly, in complete sentences, and on the text itself, so the writers who are likely to do the revision much later can remember feedback clearly and see exactly where each comment applies to the original text. This will also allow them to see repeated suggestions from more than one reader, and patterns can be quite persuasive.

- *First, everyone but the writer must speak.* Have a volunteer or two start each group session with a descriptive summary of what they have read. Then have several people share their feedback, before calling on others who are less forthcoming. Over the course of a given period of time, it is imperative students have multiple opportunities to practice speaking as a reviewer, as the reviewer gains as much from the process of feedback as the writer. Reading critically, devising constructive criticism and praise, and articulating one's critical work is irreplaceable in helping our students become confident in their textual power. Don't let students' shyness deny them the opportunity for this growth. Even if they only offer a description of the piece they read or recount what someone else has offered, this is a chance to practice critical literacy. After all, asserting descriptive and evaluative claims about texts is what we reward in academia. Students, including ELLs, need practice doing it.

- *The writer must listen.* Since writers won't sit next to every reader explaining what they meant, they need to know what real readers are and aren't getting. Don't let writers burn up this opportunity for feedback with defenses and explanations. They must be silent until the workshop is complete, except perhaps to get clarification on a piece of feedback. Afterward, they should reiterate key points of feedback and get confirmation from their reviewers. If time allows, they can share ideas about what they intended and gather feedback from peers who may have helpful suggestions about realizing original goals more effectively.

- *Writers must take "no thank you bites."* Before I let them officially dislike a food, my own children must at least take a "no thank you bite." Very often, they concede that the risk was well worth taking. In this spirit, I have students choose a suggested revision and try it. They can, of course, choose not to keep the revision, but only after they have actually seen the outcome. This doesn't mean they must take every suggestion or try out a whole text revision every time, but usually the comments echo one another enough to indicate one suggestion worth trying. Again, don't allow students to miss out on a learning opportunity by rejecting the suggestions they received out of hand.

The Culmination of Workshops: Publishing and Sharing

- *Every poet must submit.* This is a great opportunity for young writers to consider their growth, their strengths, and so forth. The selection and presentation of their best work is part of the process of submitting. It also offers teachers a good reason to teach a cover letter, so ask students to submit a formal cover letter with their best work. (Examples are widely available online.)

- *Every poet must publish.* Everyone can publish in a school or online venue, so everyone should. (Consider the NCTE National

Gallery of Writing.) Some students feign shyness or genuinely resist publishing, but anyone can at least type out a fresh copy of a single poem or a few poems, mount them in a homemade book with an introduction, and hand it in, making it a little more special than other pieces they have submitted.

- *Every poet must perform.* Every young writer should also learn to read in public. Even if your students don't plan to pursue a serious writing career, it is essential that they build their public speaking confidence and listen to their own voice sounding the piece they have written. The rehearsal process alone leads to some of the best revisions of all. Whether it is a more formal classroom reading or a full-blown slam, don't let anyone off the hook on this learning experience.

How Can We Prepare Students to Write Academic Essays with Collegiate Levels of Fluency?

Robert Scholes argues, "Our job is not to intimidate students with our own superior textual production; it is to show them the codes upon which all textual production depends, and to encourage their own textual practice" (*Textual Power* 24–25). Throughout Chapters 2 and 3, the first two practical chapters, I suggest ways in which we can develop our students' capacity to produce the meaning from text. In the last chapter, I focus on the academic benefits of critical engagement with literature.

As students explore a speaker's experience or savor a writer's choice, they are engaging in the most fundamental work of academic scholarship, interpretive close reading. As I have argued throughout the previous essays and shown through the suggested scope and sequence of the practical lessons, performing and writing creatively are not separate from but are, in my view, fundamental to the making of a truly excellent academic reader and writer. While these "creative" routes to textual power seem circuitous to some, the unique cognitive experiences and strategies students use along the way have immediate, transferable applications in traditional academic literacy across disciplines because they help students figure out how to make claims about text and support them.

Reading critically requires developing fluency in what Gerald Graff has dubbed *arguespeak*, not to mention the seemingly obscure language of literature and other disciplines in academia. Writing about one's own critical reading also requires deliberately choosing effective strategies for summarizing and communicating interpreted meaning, and supporting claims with evidence in a fluent and eloquent manner. These are the tools of the successful academic. These are the tools with which we, as English teachers, must ultimately equip our students.

But how, explicitly, do we help students do this in the 360-degree tour? Building on the thinking, discussing, and claiming that has been going on through performance and creative writing workshop activities, you can prompt students to start formalizing their claims and developing formal academic arguments. The Describing Text Templates then help students to make and support claims that make up the bulk of critical writing in the humanities. From there, plenty of practice, feedback, and reading will help students develop the sophisticated fluency that marks the college-ready student.

In the last chapter of this book, I suggest ways in which students can channel the strategies they've learned for close reading and powerful writing into academic debate and explication. Again using engaging, social, and participatory strategies for close reading and peer workshop, students will learn to write explications.

Please note, the lessons in *360 Degrees of Text* are targeted to address a subset of skills within academic composition; they are not intended to represent a plan for teaching paragraphing per se or academic composition, just claim making and textual analysis. Building upon the close reading skills established in the performance and creative writing chapters, the templates for formulating summaries, claims, and artful supporting paragraphs are tools teachers can use to move students more quickly and deliberately toward college levels of textual power, which means, as Gerald Graff and Cathy Birkenstein argue, "We need to be as explicit as possible about the key moves of academic and public-sphere literacy and helping as many students as we can to master them" ("Progressive" 16). Their bestselling book *They Say/I Say: The Moves That Matter in Academic Writing* also uses templates to help high school and college students master academic argument and was written for the explicit purpose of helping teachers help those of us who didn't just pick it up on our own.

True college readiness requires that students feel confident in their reading, their writing, and their ability to make claims. Carol Jago argues that "composing an analytical essay forces students to reread with a purpose and to scrutinize the text, as well as to analyze the author's craft. It also demands that they do this work for themselves" (3–4). Whether students are reciting or debating a poem, or composing an argument about it, the final aim of this book is procedural and metacognitive knowledge, to help all students get better at doing the work for themselves, not just answering questions generated by teachers and textbooks.

We shouldn't save the pleasures of sophisticated textual appreciation for those students willing to apprentice themselves to English teachers like me, but we should give every student the opportunity to engage in critical and authentic ways with discourse about literature and other intellectually challenging texts. Ideas about how to do this is what the 360-degree approach offers, particularly this last set of lessons.

How Can Instruction Be Differentiated within This 360-Degree Approach?

We have to work on constructing and representing meaning from the premise that both struggling and advanced students can make and support sophisticated claims about literature and that all students deserve a chance to learn how to demonstrate their ambitious exploration of texts in a variety of ways. Therefore, the scaffolding of the entire sequence and the activities built into each lesson provide many opportunities for students of all readiness levels to construct and represent meaning in various modes.

The whole sequence of sample lessons is infinitely expandable; more practice with more texts at the same or increasingly challenging levels of complexity allow for all sorts of differentiating in terms of depth and breadth for students at many access points along the way. *The text, the pace,* and *the modality* the student or teacher chooses for formative or summative assessment are also variables for differentiating instruction. Over the course of the entire sequence and within each lesson there are many ways to adjust the content (supplemental text suggestions are labeled *Widely Accessible* to most high school students, *More Difficult, Challenging*), process (select from strategies on the tour), and product (select from products on the tour). The evidence you will collect over time to assess the objective you set for students at varying levels of readiness will shape the product selection and your use of associated rubrics. The overarching sequence each student follows may be essentially the same, but the time each student takes to make the journey to explicative writing or a major performance project could vary enormously, depending on each student's level of readiness in terms of task complexity and the level of complexity in texts with which you expect students to engage.

The sample lessons are examples of how these differentiation variables can be arranged in relation to a common learning goal in order to support growth over time for every student. I believe that all the activity types are valuable to all students, and all students ought to be able to try them, though all may not be expected to achieve the same result on the same day or with the same amount of scaffolding and practice. The structured academic conversations and rich oral experiences support ELLs effectively when accessible texts are selected.

Please note, the formative assessment tasks at the end of each lesson allow teachers to check for understanding and provide feedback to students, but the lessons in the 360-degree tour are focused on practicing discrete textual analysis strategies and reflecting metacognitively upon the fruits of those strategies. Again, the 360-degree approach to text should not be treated as an approach to teaching formal academic composition in literature, only certain aspects of it. Even the suggested culminating activities need to be carefully supplemented if they are to be used as culminating or summative assessments. What tolerable evidence can you collect over time to make the claim that a student in grade 7 can "Analyze how a drama's or poem's form or structure (e.g., soliloquy, sonnet) contributes to its meaning" (Common Core)? What markers will represent progress toward those goals? These are the kinds of questions we need to be asking if we are really thinking about how to make any set of standards useful.

Note

1. Portions of this section are excerpted from my article "Nurturing the Omnivore: Approaches to Teaching Poetry," originally published by *Poetry Foundation: Learning Lab*, 13 Oct. 2009, http://www.poetryfoundation.org/learning/article/237898. Web.

II Practice

2 Teaching Close Reading through Performance and Recitation

Poems as Scripts

I have come to believe that in order to give students a real taste for poetry, we actually have to put poems into their mouths. We can't leave poetic texts hanging aloft, as lifeless totems, understood and worshipped only by leaders of some literary tribe. Instead, through performance strategies, we can offer students a chance to sample the fruits of poetic texts, bringing all sorts of readers at all levels of readiness to the table.

Speaking poetry out loud, "with feeling," to use the old cliché, helps students cultivate an expert kind of appreciation. By adopting a performance stance, readers explore the voices and images invoked by text as they endeavor to embody the speakers, inhabit their worlds, and ultimately represent the text's meaning to an audience. As a result, they become authentic meaning makers, considering aspects of language that might have gone unnoticed in silent reading or textbook questioning. This intimate exploration of text can make visible the painstaking work of the artist and raise questions about multiple possible meanings that change as the text is intoned in various ways by diverse readers

Rather than acting as experts who can assure students who have never tasted it that a poem is delicious, we can challenge students to use performance as a strategy for understanding. When we do this, we recast their epistemological roles, inviting them into our tribe of meaning makers who can savor poems for themselves.

This set of lessons is intended to license teachers to help students develop sophisticated close reading skills through genuinely engaging, imagination-driven strategies. Given the impetus of group performance and ultimately individual recitation, students will learn to visualize, think aloud, and engage in other imaginative acts to perform more skilled close readings. They will learn to identify the key components of a rhetorical situation—context, speaker, occasion, audience, purpose, genre, subject, and tone—approach texts in search of an antecedent scenario, divide texts into smaller parts for more skilled structural analysis, and, of course, paraphrase texts faithfully. Each of these strategies can be deployed in any reading situation, helping students gain a confidence of control over even the most complex texts. Performing poems is a learning strategy. The processes required to prepare a performance promote the development of skills that effective readers employ in close reading and analytical writing later.

The culminating lesson challenges students to practice all of these strategies introduced and to explore the emotional structure of a poem from the inside out. After all of the earlier modeling and practice in large and small groups, the final recitation assignment provides opportunities for students to engage independently and critically with a text of their choice. Recitation itself is added to their repertoire of strategies!

A special note about "close reading" extension activities: Every lesson on the 360-degree tour prepares students to make written claims about text. At the end of each lesson, where ideas for extending the work are provided, I have shared a close-reading writing prompt in the form of a fill-in-the-blank paragraph-starting claim about the poem highlighting the particular focus of the lesson. In the final chapter, those training wheels will be removed, and students are challenged to make independent claims about any aspect of any poem; but throughout these initial lessons, it is important for students to practice this focused critical reading, writing, and thinking.

Lesson 1: Visualizing and Thinking about Persona

Teacher-to-Teacher Note. Playing with language and sharing important personal experiences are necessary steps in establishing a culture that allows for optimal collaboration in learning. On the first day, invite students to sit in a circle on the floor. Tell students they will return to this circle throughout their study of poetry, as they collaborate as readers, writers, and performers. Establish this as a special place and, to the extent it is possible, help students overcome aversions to sitting on the floor. Help students understand that this circle is a place where everyone is equal and everyone can play, make mistakes, and enjoy language. This lesson also serves as a trust-building exercise, which is a critical component of performing, discussing, and writing about poetry.

The first exercise was adapted from an exercise I learned at DePaul University in an NEH-sponsored seminar called "Saying Something Wonderful: Teaching the Pleasures of Poetry." I have used it with great success with diverse populations of students for years. In the exercise, students become familiar with the concept of persona by carefully selecting and arranging images to prepare ad hoc stories about themselves. Later you will point out that poets and other writers create personas for their speakers through a similar process of selecting and presenting details.

The subject of this storytelling activity also lays the thematic groundwork for the poem in the sample lesson. However, because the subject has to do with overcoming an obstacle, be prepared for a range of responses from the mundane to the dramatic. Given the nature of youth and their personal lives, it is also important to contract with them in the same way you would when you assign journal entries, reminding them of your professional obligations and their own obligations as members of a supportive learning community.

Lesson Step 1.1: Sharing a Moment of Overcoming

1. Before students enter class for this first lesson, create a display for the term *rhetorical situation* with this working definition: a context in which there is an act of communication. Helpful graphics of the rhetorical triangle are readily available online. Also create a display of the words that make up the acronym SOAPSTone. (For each rhetorical situation, there is a context as well as a <u>S</u>peaker/author/communicator, an <u>O</u>ccasion for speaking, an <u>A</u>udience, a <u>P</u>urpose, and a <u>S</u>ubject that shape the speaker's <u>Tone</u>.) You can also distribute the SOAPSTone student handout (handout 1.A found in the appendix) and have students keep it in their in-class notebooks. Make these displays permanent for student reference.

2. Tell students they will be sharing a one-minute story of a time when they overcame an obstacle. Think, for example, of an accomplishment, facing a fear, finding the right outfit, a spill in aisle four, or the like. The stories can be funny, thought-provoking, surprising—anything students feel comfortable sharing.

3. Rather than simply explaining, demonstrate how each person will enter the circle with a physical gesture that evokes an image from the story (for example, throwing a baseball, striking a disco pose, etc.). Explain that once in the center of the circle, the person must wait five beats before speaking. Raise your hand and count five fingers silently. The person in the circle will then tell their story as vividly as possible. When finished, the speaker will wait while you again count five silent beats with your fingers before leaving the circle. As a supportive leader and co-learner, you should demonstrate a telling of your own story as you explain the exercises. Your subject choice and your commitment to full participation in the activity will go a long way toward establishing your credibility as a learning leader.

4. After one or two minutes of silent, individual brainstorming, ask for a volunteer to begin. When volunteers stop raising their hands, assure the bashful that there is no right or wrong, worthy or unworthy story, simply a recounting of a time of overcoming

an obstacle. Then proceed by going clockwise from the last volunteer until everyone has shared. This is a "mandatory volunteer" process I like. In my experience, even the toughest, most reserved participants cave in eventually.

5. After everyone has shared a story, ask students to pair up and share the experience of this storytelling activity using the following questions: How was your selection of your subject and its details shaped by concerns about how your audience of peers would perceive you, the speaker? How did the gesture focus our attention?

6. In a large group debrief, ask a few pairs to share some of the factors that shaped the storytelling experience. Segue to the idea of the rhetorical situation. After explaining that the students created texts (that is, the stories they shared) in a particular context that shaped what story was selected and which details were shared in which order, let them know that as they explore the rhetorical situation in each of the poems they'll read, they will learn to begin determining the gist of texts, any text, by identifying key elements of the rhetorical situation, such as audience, purpose or genre, and context. Refer again to your display of the rhetorical triangle and SOAPSTone questions. Highlight the ways in which student stories were selected and shaped based on the context of their peer audience, and emphasize that one of the key concerns that storytellers had was how the story would shape their audience's perception of the storyteller's persona, as a person who is funny, smart, and so on. After all, no one is more conscious of their audience's perception of their persona than an adolescent.

Lesson Step 1.2: Discovering Persona through Visualizing Images

In this lesson step, students will practice the habit of visualizing—one by one—the concrete images the speaker of a poem selects and arranges. Students will practice getting the gist of a poem by *seeing* imagery in written texts the same way they *see* images in a visual text. Throughout this process, they will become familiar with the speaker, in this case the persona Maya Angelou has created in the poem "Still I Rise." They will share their findings through a theatrical technique of sculpting a portrait of the speaker, where a student performer becomes the clay to be sculpted. For reliable editions of the text, see "Additional Resources for Chapter 2" at the end of the chapter.

Teacher-to-Teacher Note. Reading Maya Angelou's "Still I Rise" as a portrait of a speaker will reveal Angelou's process of selecting and arranging images to convey a particular persona. In my experience, students really love this poem and enjoy the way in which Angelou uses imagery to develop the persona of an individual person who has overcome struggle in order to comment on the collective experience of Africans and African Americans.

1. *Frontloading Knowledge Option:* Have students develop expert groups to research Maya Angelou's biography, the transatlantic slave trade, and timelines of African American migration history to learn about possible sources for her imagery.

2. Remind students that they selected and arranged images for their own stories for the purpose of presenting a certain image of themselves, a persona, to the classroom audience. Likewise, the author of a poem creates a particular persona through the careful selection and arrangement of images, and in order to really see this portrait, we have to visualize the images she selected. In discussing poetry, remember that the speaker is not always the author, though in some cases the author's speaker can bear a resemblance.

3. Many images of Maya Angelou are available on the Internet illustrating her multifaceted identity as an African American thinker, artist, leader, dancer, educator and poet; share two or three of these with students. The portraits show a range of personas that Angelou adopts for various occasions. Give students a moment to assign key adjectives one might use to describe the persona she projects in each image; ask them to indicate orally or in writing which detail or aspect of the image caused them to make that judgment. Highlight the fact that your questioning helped them examine their own thinking, and that this metacognitive thinking is what strong, critical readers do.

4. Distribute Key Literary Terms for Discussing Imagery and Think-Aloud Prompts (see student handouts 1.B and 1.C in the appendix). Explain to students that just as they were able to describe the persona in these visual images, they will learn to visualize images in text and make claims about how a poet creates a persona by selecting and arranging certain details in a particular way. Point out that just as they were able to identify key parts of the visual images, which are simply visual texts, they will need to learn how to "see" key parts of verbal texts and describe them in a common language so others can understand what prompted a particular interpretation. To do this more effectively, explain that as a community of learners, they need a common language for describing text. Let them know that the language you are asking them to use in these discussions is also good practice for the advanced reading and writing they will do later, since texts about texts employ these terms. If this is your students' first encounter with either of these concepts, assure them that you will model this kind of speaking before asking them to use it. This is essential for ELLs.

5. Segue into modeling a think-aloud by explaining that you will be asking students to think out loud with peers as a way of

developing awareness about the impact of personal experience, context, and an author's choices on a reader's interpretation of a text. Let them know that the think-aloud prompts will remind them to perform expert reader moves on the text, and that if they practice them enough, they will see the fruits of those metacognitive moves and adopt them as habits for life.

6. Model a think-aloud using Maya Angelou's poem, "Still I Rise." Read the poem out loud. Then prompt students to practice visualizing images in the first stanza, creating pictures of the speaker in their mind. Tell them that they will have a chance to visualize each image in the poem carefully with their peers, but that they will need to talk about their thinking each step of the way. Below is a sample of how I think aloud about the first stanza with my students after reading the entire poem aloud once:

> <u>Well, based on her diction, a.k.a. her word choice, I am guessing</u> that she must be pretty annoyed with the person who wrote her down with "bitter," "twisted lies."Listen to those adjectives! <u>I know how it makes me feel when</u> someone lies about me.
>   <u>I am puzzled by the fact</u> that she would compare herself to dust in the simile in the last line. Dust <u>makes me picture</u> something dirty. That doesn't seem like a flattering comparison.
>   But, when I think about the gist of the poem and read things later like "up from the past rooted in pain / I rise," it makes me think this person sounds powerful and resilient. <u>It makes me wonder,</u> what about dust would be good for showing her resilience or power?

For a visual demonstration of this simile, I grab any number of dusty or chalky things in my room and clap them together. I hope I'm not the only one with these classroom resources on hand! After a mental visualization or a demonstration, the students should note how powerful and ubiquitous dust can be, how the act of stamping dust down makes it rise more and more. Wrap up this model think-aloud by highlighting the importance of careful visualization, and ask students to reflect upon the effectiveness of the dust visual in understanding the simile.

7. Arrange students in eight small groups, assigning one stanza per group. Have them read through the whole poem and practice thinking aloud about how they visualize images. Have them select only one Think-Aloud Prompt to try if necessary, but make sure they use it. Encourage students to practice the suggested Think-Aloud Prompts with the first few stanzas. Have them zero in on their assigned stanza, and have everyone sketch what they see before sharing findings with their group. Tell them to note the words and phrases that are evoked by the images. Use

Key Literary Terms for Discussing Imagery (handout 1.B in the appendix) as you circulate, asking questions such as the following: What are the <u>details</u> in this stanza? What do those <u>images</u> make you picture? What was it about her <u>diction</u>—the words she chooses—that was striking to you? Why do you think she chose that <u>metaphor/simile</u>? Which qualities of . . . would be shared by . . . in this metaphor or simile?

8. Ask each group to share what they visualized, noting the words and phrases evoked by the visual image. Praise students for their precise use of Key Literary Terms for Discussing Imagery as they share their findings. Then ask the whole group to consider what claims can be made about the identity of the speaker and her purpose for speaking. To close this larger group discussion, ask a few students to share the gist of the poem as they see it, just a quick summary that answers the SOAPSTone questions. A formal written response to the SOAPSTone questions could also be collected for assessment purposes, but the important thing here is that students get used to seeing text through this rhetorical situation lens.

Lesson Step 1.3: Sculpting a Silent Portrait

1. Tell students that their next job is to select a group member to act as a piece of sculpting clay. In groups, using their stanza, have students sculpt a portrait of the speaker that is a fitting portrayal of the persona Angelou creates. Remind them to balance the specificity of the image with the general portrayal of this speaker, so the audience can see the underlying coherence of the poem, while savoring the details that help make the portrayal of this persona richer. (Allow students to determine the role of group members in speaking, sculpting, and acting as clay. Equality among ensemble members leads to wonderful critical debates in more elaborate performances of poems, so it is a great time to lay the groundwork for ensemble by avoiding such roles as director, actor, etc.)

2. After a few minutes of theatrical play and the eventual distribution of roles, have students return to the circle, strike their poses, and share their impromptu performances.

3. After enjoying the performances, discuss new revelations about the poem, the speaker, and the process of reading this way to remind students to be aware that they are acquiring new and valid strategies (visualization, think-aloud, and annotation), and theatrical improvisation. They will use these tools independently in performances later.

4. For homework, give students a piece of construction paper and ask them to compose a single vivid image (one line) and illustrate it for a whole class poem called "Still I Rise." Using as a starting

point the artful form of a simile (Like _____, I rise) or a metaphor (I am _____, I rise), ask students to use concrete words to create a *vivid visual* image, something we can picture in our minds, to complete the phrase. They may choose to use an image from the story they shared during their first day in the circle or an entirely new one—perhaps one inspired by Angelou's work. Encourage students to draft on another sheet of paper, revise, and record their final version on the construction paper you provide.

If time allows, students may listen to a masterful performance by one of my former students on Chicago Public Radio's *Eight Forty-Eight,* available at http://www.wbez.org/episode-segments/speak#. After listening, students should discuss their take on the performer's perception of the speaker.

Lesson Step 1.4: Arranging Images

1. Have students join the circle, bringing their vivid images printed clearly on construction paper. As students share their contributions to the whole class poem, have them discuss their images and reasons for choosing them. Highlight the relationship between the ideas the images evoke and how the details of the text shape those images in particular ways.

2. Next, have everyone stand up and hold their piece of construction paper in front of them. Have students read their piece aloud in a round robin of the whole poem, allowing nervous students the option of exchanging with another writer for the read-aloud. After reading, give students one minute to silently group themselves in the circle according to their images; for example, the students who used a nature image might all see a connection to each other. Debrief the reasons for these arrangements and decide on the final one. In the closing discussion, have students consider how the arrangement of an image within the larger text impacts its meaning. Post the poem inside the classroom for future reference—good examples of vivid imagery, similes, and metaphors!

3. Wrap up this discussion by reminding students that through visualization strategies they can begin to get the gist of even terribly difficult poems. Add that taking the time to visualize images and to think about their own thinking is essential for close reading and good writing. Assure students that they will grow more comfortable with the use of the language of literature as they practice using it and that the language itself will become a key to understanding text, not just a vocabulary for describing it.

More Poems for Practice

For more practice with visualizing details to explore persona, use "Hook" by James Wright (widely accessible), "Bilingual/Bilingue" by Rhina P.

Espaillat (more difficult), or "Mirror" by Sylvia Plath (challenging). To assess students at lower levels of readiness, collect illustrations of one poem or a part of a poem in which students include a sentence completion based on a think-aloud prompt, such as "This makes me picture . . . because when I think of . . . I think of. . . ." On-level students can complete evidence-supported SOAPSTones, while students who are advanced may use the notes in their SOAPSTones to write paragraphs in which they describe the persona of the speaker, using Think-Aloud Prompts as sentence starters and making specific references to the text to support answers.

More Close Reading, Performance, and Powerful Writing Ideas

Close Reading

Have students read at least three other poems by Maya Angelou. Then have them complete and support the following claim sentence in a paragraph that is supported by evidence from the text: "Maya Angelou often uses images of _____ to depict speakers who _____." (For example, "Maya Angelou often uses images of triumph to depict speakers who have overcome great obstacles.")

Performance

Have students perform an Angelou poem as a group. Help students prepare by considering the following questions: What images are dominant in the poem? What are the variations on these dominant images? To whom does the speaker speak and why? What gestures would she use? What tone of voice does she use and how does it change, image to image?

Artful Writing

Students may use the "Still I Rise" homework assignment as a basis for an entire poem or use the title and write a brief vignette about a moment of struggle or overcoming.

Lesson 2: Dividing Poems into Parts and Determining Antecedent Scenarios

Teacher-to-Teacher Note. Students have gained some valuable insights into the creation of a poem—especially how a poet creates a persona through the selection and arrangement of vivid images. Using the visualization and think-aloud techniques they learned in the first lesson and a new technique, dividing poems into smaller parts, students will explore the ways in which a poet also uses concrete images to create narratives.

Students will also use Key Literary Terms for Discussing Imagery to practice asking questions about the antecedent scenario; that is, what happened before the poem that made this speaker speak in this way at this time. Through the technique of role-playing, students will then present a performance of Sharon Olds's "I Go Back to May 1937," showing how the images of the poem reveal an intense family history. For reliable sources of the text, see "Additional Resources for Chapter 2" at the end of the chapter. Before the lesson, have students bring in an old family photo.

Lesson Step 2.1: Introducing "I Go Back to May 1937" with Old Photos

1. *Frontloading Knowledge Option:* Like visual art, narrative poems often tell a story without using the traditional markers found in prose that allow us to identify exact chronology or explicit events. Ask students to determine possible antecedent scenarios and probable outcomes in the narrative captured in the details of an image, using a photo like the movie poster for the film *Life Begins at College* found at http://cinema.americanfootballitalia.com/myPictures/1937LIFEBEGINSATCOLLEGE2.jpg. After students generate ideas and defend their answers with references to the images, ask them to consider what outside information they have used to make these judgments. Challenge them to consider how their readings were influenced by love story narratives that are constantly reinforced in our culture. Use this example to highlight how, in addition to knowledge that the author provides, readers connect their own experiences or experiences with certain storylines that are familiar to us all, such as a love story, childbirth, or tales of unhappy marriages to make meaning. Segue into their family photos with the closing discussion about how we might bring knowledge of these kinds of stories to our own lives as well, often viewing our lives through the lens of these archetypal stories.

2. Have students perform a quick-write describing the thoughts, feelings, and conclusions about the people in the picture that were evoked by the family photo that they selected, and then ask students to share with a partner. In a large group debrief, have students share the ways in which family stories or more general culturally significant stories about human experience influenced their experience of the photo. You might ask, for example, how do you use stories that are familiar to all of us (archetypal stories) to fill in the blanks about the people inside and outside the photo when you were not there?

3. Distribute the poem "I Go Back to May 1937" by Sharon Olds and have students visualize the images as you read the text aloud. Read it aloud again. As you read the second time, students should play back the movie already created by the mind's eye, adding more detail this time to each mental image (Wilhelm, *Reading* 42).

4. After a third read-aloud, do what I call an "I'll do it first, then we'll do it together" think-aloud with the first five lines. Here is a sample:

> Based on a couple of readings of the poem, <u>the speaker seems</u> to be looking at pictures. The first couple of lines are making me picture the photograph of the father. <u>I am picturing</u> an old-fashioned sort of college because of the stone arch. <u>The details make</u> me think the picture is in color, because she says the tiles are red. <u>I am puzzled by the simile</u> "like bent / plates of blood."

Stop and, if possible, have several students use the metaphor / simile prompt to think aloud with you. Allow time to think about the diction, prompting students with questions about the realm of discourse in which they have heard the words "plates of blood."

> <u>That simile makes me associate</u> something about the picture with biology because when most people think about plates of blood, they picture . . .

Together, students can help unpack the idea of imperfection (bent), hemorrhaging (blood), and bloodline / heredity and disease (plates of blood as studied under a microscope). It is a great time to highlight that writers often borrow terms from other realms of discourse in order to help readers draw on their experience and knowledge of other things to make multiple associations. Encourage students to pay special attention to this Think-Aloud Prompt: This metaphor / simile / image makes me associate _____ with _____ because when most people think of _____, they think of _____.

5. Have students work in small groups to imagine the speaker's persona, applying the strategies they have already learned (visualization, think-aloud, illustration, and annotation / note-taking). This time, however, tell them the purpose of their reading is to figure out what might have happened before the poem began. What situation prompted this speaker to speak at this moment? In Helen Vendler's words, what is the antecedent scenario (*Poems, Poets, Poetry*)?

6. After students have carefully investigated the text, share a projection of the entire text for the class. Have several groups share their take on the *antecedent scenario*. Ask what happened that might have made this speaker utter these words. Prompt students to reference specific lines and phrases from the text to support their claims by asking, "What words or phrases made you think that?"

7. Explain that in order to get deeper into the poem, they will now add another trick to their repertoire of close reading techniques—dividing the poem into parts. Ask students, "If I were to break this poem into parts to make my close reading of each part a little

easier to handle, where would the breaks come?" Individually or in small groups, have students draw lines between main sections of the poem. On the master copy, have a few students share where to place a line to indicate each division. Have them explain why they believe there was a change from one major part to the next (changes might be indicated by a change in image, time, action, idea, or emotion). Praise students for their use of key terms and specific references to the text and for effective summarizing and putting things into their own words faithfully (that is, paraphrasing).

Lesson Step 2.2: Creating Talking Sculptures

1. Have small groups dramatize the text to portray the antecedent scenario as it is depicted in the text using these techniques: *Silent sculpture* (see lesson step 1.3, "Sculpting a Silent Portrait"), *tableau vivant* (an arrangement of silent sculptures in a living mural) and *talking sculptures* (the sculptures come alive at different points in the performance of the text, when various characters have something to say). Each group will use the images and words of the text to develop an ad hoc performance that takes the audience on a journey through the family's story, stopping at different points in time to hear from each character.

2. Here are some questions students may consider while preparing roles for talking sculptures:

   - What would the father and mother in the photo say about themselves, their futures, and their relationship at the moment these pictures were taken?

   - What scenes in their later lives does the text conjure?

   - What images of the speaker's experience with these characters are embedded in the text (the speaker's younger selves, her self at the moment of the text)? How are younger and older images of this speaker the same or different?

   Students may need more or less direction, depending on their willingness to play with these improvisational techniques.

   More Improvisational Ideas: Groups may use mime in the background or have various characters vocalize their imagined scenarios in concert with the poem. They may have characters tap in/tap out to show changes in the character. (For example, an actor walks up to a character and taps that person, indicating the actor should freeze, while the new actor assumes the predecessor's pose and carries on with the part.)

3. After performances, have the students discuss how the poet selected and arranged images to tell the complicated story of this embattled family in this brief poem.

More Poems for Practice

Have students practice visualizing, looking for antecedent scenarios, dividing poems into parts, and annotating with other narrative poems, including "Jenny Kiss'd Me" by Leigh Hunt (widely accessible), "Theme for English B" by Langston Hughes (more difficult), and "My Last Duchess" by Robert Browning (challenging).

For a quick assessment of students at lower levels of readiness, have students practice visualizing the story of one of these poems and then describing the events of the story in a couple of sentences. Have them use key transition words (such as *first, second, third*) to indicate the sequence of events. On-level students should first visualize a poem, making notes in the right margin, and then read to discover the antecedent scenario, making notes on the left side. Using lines on their annotated copies of the poem, students should also divide the poem into parts and indicate their dividing principle (images changed, time changed, etc.). Advanced students may be further challenged metacognitively by writing a reflection on the differences each approach to the reading made. They should use evidence from their own notations to support their claims about how reading to visualize versus reading to discover the antecedent scenario approach produced different results.

More Close Reading, Performance, and Powerful Writing Ideas

Close Reading Sharon Olds

Using titles suggested in *More Poems for Practice,* have students complete and support the following claim sentence: "_____, the author of _____, reveals the story of a speaker who _____ by using images that suggest he or she was _____." (Sample: Sharon Olds, the author of "I Go Back to May 1937," reveals the story of a speaker who struggles with her parents' failed marriage by using images that suggest she was a victim of their unhappiness.)

Performance

Using the close reading techniques they have learned so far, students can submit a visual montage in a media of their choice of a narrative poem of their choice.

Artful Writing

Using a family photo as a prompt, have students write a poem in which they speak to the photo or the photo speaks to them. Using artful word choice (diction) and the careful selection and arrangement of details (figurative language, metaphor/simile), ask students to convey the images they see as well as the emotions the photo conjures.

Lesson 3: Paraphrasing and Analyzing Arguments

Teacher-to-Teacher Note. This lesson allows students to practice all of the skills they have learned so far, especially those developed through practice with the strategies of visualizing images, determining the antecedent scenario, and dividing the poem into parts. Students will review the concept of the rhetorical situation, noting how authors draw on the context of larger cultural narratives—about slavery in "Still I Rise," marriage in "I Go Back to May 1937," and now romance in "To His Coy Mistress"—in shaping a reader's experience. At the end of this lesson, groups will present a "slide show" of significant images of one stanza using tableau, a group of carefully posed silent sculptures (Wilhelm, *Action Strategies* 127). Students will be introduced to argumentative appeals. I have used the vocabulary *ethos*, *pathos*, and *logos* in the lesson description. However, if this vocabulary is unfamiliar, students can discuss these concepts as appeals that strengthen one's own credibility, appeals to emotions, and appeals to logic. (For more on ethos, pathos, and logos, see OWL at Purdue: http://owl.english.purdue.edu/owl/resource/588/04/.)

For reliable sources of the text, see "Additional Resources for Chapter 2" at the end of the chapter.

Lesson Step 3.1: Introducing Claims and Arguments through "To His Coy Mistress" by Andrew Marvel

Depending upon the amount of available time and the proficiency of students, steps 3.1 and 3.2 can be completed individually at home. Also, while the poem can be read and enjoyed without knowledge of words like *Ganges* and *Humber*, words like these throughout the poem offer wonderful opportunities for study: "What does *Ganges* mean?" "Why did he select the image of this river rather than another?" "What on earth does he mean by 'vegetable' love?" With time and Internet access or a glossary, students can incorporate research on the British Empire in India, etymology, and allusion in their close readings.

1. *Frontloading Knowledge Option:* Before reading, review various persuasive appeals and then have students share the lyrics to their favorite love song with a small group. Using a five-column grid in which students can list each song, the speaker, his or her goal, his or her audience, and his or her appeals, ask students to analyze the features of typical love songs. What does the speaker hope to get or achieve by singing this song? What kind of persona does the speaker typically create for himself or herself? What

claims does the speaker usually make about himself or herself? What kinds of appeals? Have students write a line or two from the song to support each claim.

Using a graphic image of the rhetorical triangle, have students deepen their understanding in a large group debrief of typical characteristics defining each aspect of the rhetorical triangle in love songs. For example, the author/speaker is usually in love, the audience is usually the beloved, and so on. The purpose is often to woo the beloved or to reconcile with him or her.

Point out that readers bring genre knowledge to readings, whether they are grocery lists or love poems, and that this kind of knowledge can be really helpful in tackling tough texts. Guessing that a tough poem fits into a familiar genre can help them navigate texts because even though sometimes the language can appear to be so old as to seem foreign, genre knowledge, such as the typical features of a love poem, can help them get the gist of a text, even before they can decode it to the point of being able to visualize, guess at the antecedent scenario, and ultimately divide it into parts for deeper analysis.

2. Tell students that in addition to the close reading techniques they have practiced, they will add another to their repertoire of strategies: paraphrasing, or putting the poem into their own words faithfully. Students will try reading "To His Coy Mistress" on their own to determine the gist of it. After sharing an example of paraphrasing, have them work in groups to paraphrase the entire poem. Have them take turns simply reading it aloud, making sense of what they can, and generating questions. Here is what I share as an example of paraphrase. I have also inserted my think-aloud commentary in parentheses for the first few lines of the poem.

Original	Paraphrase
Had we but world enough, and time, This coyness, lady, were no crime.	If we had all the time in the world Acting shy would not be a bad thing to do to me (Think aloud: *Crime? That's an interesting word choice! Is it against the law to resist his advances?*)
We would sit down and think which way To walk, and pass our long love's day;	We would sit around thinking about what to do with our time together
Thou by the Indian Ganges' side Shouldst rubies find;	You could be by that big river in India finding rubies (Think aloud: *I had to look up what the Indian Ganges was. I found out…*)
I by the tide Of Humber would complain.	I could be here by the shore in England complaining that you are gone (*I am picturing a drama king here . . . is he really overwhelmed with grief as he imagines being away from her? I'm not sure if I trust him yet. I'll give him the benefit of the doubt until I read on.*)

3. After students complete their paraphrasing, bring the whole group back together and refer to the SOAPSTone display in the classroom. After identifying the poem's SOAPSTone as a class, have a few groups share their paraphrases.

Lesson Step 3.2: Creating a Slide Show

1. Divide the class into three groups. Have students prepare a performance of a single stanza of the poem, *using every member of the group and every group member's voice.* Tell them the goal of this ad hoc performance is to highlight the speaker's intentions and his strategic use of appeals to ethos (the speaker's own credibility,) logos (the mistress's logic or reason), and pathos (the mistress's emotions), as well as the mistress's possible response to each image in the speaker's argument. To that end, they will choose two or three images that best capture their take on the stanza. They will create a silent physicalization, a "Slide Show" using these images (Wilhelm, *Action Strategies* 127). Performances should take place in the circle, moving fluently from one stanza (group) to the next.

2. Debrief the performances, asking groups to discuss the speaker's appeals and the mistress's possible responses. Ask how this poem is similar and different from the typical love songs we hear today.

3. Have students return to their groups for deeper analysis of their parts, labeling what they think the speaker is doing in each movement of his persuasive argument (flattering, impressing, pressuring, convincing, etc.). Write the following sentence stem on the board as a speaking prompt: "When the speaker chooses to say _____, it seems as though he is appealing to (ethos, logos, or pathos) because he uses the image of _____, which he feels will cause the mistress to _____." Have students use this lens to guide their analyses. As always, be sure to model Key Literary Terms for Discussing Imagery.

4. In a large group debrief, ask students to share claims about the speaker's tactics in developing the argument, using the sentence stem to prompt fluent and precise claims about the text.

5. After sharing these claims about the speaker's argument, let students know that they too have made an argument by making claims about the speaker's choices and that these interpretive claims are the basis of arguments about literature.

More Poems for Practice

Other poems that may be used to complete all of the activities outlined here include "The Bait" by John Donne, "The Passionate Shepherd to

His Love" by Christopher Marlowe, and "The Nymph's Reply to the Shepherd" by Sir Walter Raleigh. These poems are all fairly challenging. Students at lower levels of readiness may need a great deal of scaffolding to paraphrase them. This activity can be extended by asking students to describe what might have happened prior to this moment to make this speaker say these things at this time as well as how the speaker attempts to make himself or herself appealing to his or her audience. On-level students can paraphrase one of the suggested poems in this lesson and look at the argument through the lens of ethos, pathos, and logos, making written claims about the poem. Advanced students may read "Coy Mistress" by Annie Finch (found at http://www.poetryfoundation.org/archive/poem.html?id=175353), paraphrase the poem to determine the gist of Finch's counterargument, and write a brief analysis of how Finch responds to various aspects of Marvel's choices in her response poem.

More Close Reading, Performance, and Powerful Writing Ideas

Close Reading

Have students complete this claim and support it with evidence from the text: "The image that might have been most/least effective in the speaker's persuasive argument to his mistress was the image of _____, which is captured in the line _____ because it suggests that _____." This prompt may also be applied to any of the titles in *More Poems for Practice*. (Sample: The image that might have been least effective in the speaker's persuasive argument to his mistress was the image of her beauty being destroyed by death, which is captured in the line "thy beauty shall no more be found" because it suggests that, in his view, her beauty is only external and will pass.)

Performance

Have students record music-video style performances of one of the poems discussed in this lesson.

Artful Writing

Students can rewrite the Marvel poem or the coy mistress's response using a modern speaker and modern words.

Lesson 4: Determining the Emotional Moves

Teacher-to-Teacher Note. The culminating lesson challenges students to recite a poem of their own choosing. This recitation assignment can be used as the basis for future recitation assignments. Using "Facing It" by Yusef Komunyakaa, students will explore how one might determine the emotional moves of a poem in the course of preparing a performance. For reliable copies of the poem, see "Additional Resources for Chapter 2" at the end of the chapter.

Lesson Step 4.1: Introducing "Facing It" by Yusef Komunyakaa

1. *Frontloading Knowledge Option:* Provide or have students find or develop brief (no more than a paragraph) encyclopedic entries about Andrew Johnson, the Vietnam War, the Civil Rights Movement, and Maya Lin.

   Introduce the phrase *associated meanings*, saying that as individual readers, we make unique connections between the text and knowledge and experiences we carry in our minds. We associate images with certain feelings or previous experience with common symbolic uses of particular images, just as we associate our ideas about typical kinds of stories with stories within the same genre. For example, we associate images of warmth with good feelings and images of physical coldness with discomfort.

   In this poem, students will find that the poet may be playing with references to specific historical events, famous people, and even phrases that we, as part of the English language community or American culture, agree have a few distinct meanings. Give the students an example of this last category by projecting the following sentence stem: When most people think of the phrase *face it*, they think _____ or they think _____. After filling in the blanks individually, have students share possible associations with the phrase. Explain that they will use the poem "Facing It" to learn how to prepare a formal recitation, using the same careful attention to language that they have been practicing throughout group performance work and close reading activities.

2. Display a visual of the Vietnam Veterans Memorial prior to the lesson (see "Additional Resources for Chapter 2" for image sources). As you display the image, share the following background with students: Maya Lin, a young architecture student at Yale University, designed the Vietnam Memorial in Washington, D.C. The memorial, which was constructed in 1982 on the Washington Mall between the Lincoln Memorial and the Washington Monument, invites visitors to step inside a 10□-foot wall, which expands laterally, several hundred feet from its vertex. It sinks six feet below the horizon. The two black granite wings open like a book, inside of which the name of every fallen soldier is engraved. (I typically

then invite students to share personal encounters with the monument before introducing the poem.) Yusef Komunyakaa, himself a Vietnam veteran, explores the impact of this sacred place upon its visitors in his poem "Facing It." (I also have a black granite cheese plate that I pass around before reading. Though it isn't essential, seeing the reflective quality of polished granite really helps students visualize the scene more vividly. Small samples of polished granite are sometimes available at hardware and tile stores.)

3. Share the poem, and start students off by doing a think-aloud, again using the "I'll do it first, then we'll do it together" model. You do the first two lines, and then have students help you do the next two. Here is how I think aloud about the first section.

> I have this picture of the speaker facing the memorial. I am picturing an African American speaker, because he says "my black face fades," but then he says his face is "hiding inside the black granite," so maybe his reflection just looks shadowy, or maybe he means "black" more figuratively, as in sad. See, that is another example of associated meanings. Look how many things I thought about when I saw that word repeated. I don't know; I'll have to come back to that. I think I'll circle the word black, since it is used twice, and I'll jot down the question, "why does he repeat black?" I always note repetitions and variations because those patterns usually tell me something.
> I wonder why he is using the word "hiding." It is an interesting word choice, because it makes it seem like his reflection has a mind of its own, like it is another live version of himself. I am going to circle that too.

Ask students to help with a think-aloud about the next two lines. Ask: "What questions run through your mind as you read the next two lines?" Have several students share. They will probably point out that he seems to be upset; some students may even note that the speaker seems to have predicted that he would be upset with the line, "I said I wouldn't." After allowing several students to share their contributions you may jump back in, building on student responses.

> He seems to be upset, almost uncontrollably, because he says, "dammit. No tears," as if he is trying to keep from crying. I wonder why he wants to avoid crying. I wonder what he is "facing."

Once you have moved to this larger question, segue to the close reading activity, which involves thinking-aloud about the poet's choices and drawing pictures of the images in the text.

4. Project a model or provide an actual handout for sketching illustrations. The handout can be very simple: three large boxes, laid out horizontally with space beneath each box for students to

record captions or quotes from the poem pertaining to the sketch. Tell them that they will sketch key images from the text, almost like snapshots from a movie of the poem. Have students begin a close reading by asking what the speaker literally sees as he stands before the wall. Encourage them to visualize and describe every image in a think-aloud, noting especially those images that are repeated. Have them sketch what they see in sequence. Assure students that they need not create works of art, just some way to represent what they see in their mind's eye.

5. Circulate around the room, modeling Key Literary Terms for Discussing Imagery, and encourage students to use the Think-Aloud Prompts. Encourage students to walk through the physical experience to imagine the speaker's vantage point at any given moment in the poem, and ask them to draw what they see. As students are finishing up, make another round, asking, "What do you make of the way he arranges these images sequentially in the living mural he creates? Consider the location of images in relation to other images. For example, how do images of himself relate sequentially to images of others at the memorial, the outside world, and so forth?" Students may begin to literally see in their sketches how the memorial has prompted the speaker first to reflect on himself—his personal experience—and then to move outward from the experiences of other visitors to the universal experience of war, death, loss, and the like.

6. Display this question on the board: "Based on his selection and arrangement of images, what does the author suggest this speaker is 'facing' when he visits this place?" Ask students to write a brief response and then to share their answers in a large group debrief. Try to have as many students respond as possible, even if they only use brief phrases. As they share their findings, they may also refer to their illustrations and research into key terms, and so on. Have them take additional notes on the margins of the text.

Lesson Step 4.2: Creating a Tableau

1. Divide the class in two and have each half of the class arrange themselves in a "tableau" (a living mural made up of silent sculptures of multiple figures) that represents the poem. Have students focus on the goal of communicating their take on Komunyakaa's selection and arrangement of images. Ask, "How does he use these images to reveal the monument's personal, political, and cultural meaning and the effect it has on visitors?"

2. Have students present their tableau in the circle. Then, after all the performances, have students share their reasons for each of their performance choices in a large group debrief. You should begin using the word *claim* in your discussions with students if

you haven't already. Also, model claim making as you respond to student contributions, saying, "so you claim that when Komunyakaa chose this image, he was suggesting that . . . because you associated . . . with. . . ." As always, as students present their work verbally to the larger group, encourage them to use the Key Literary Terms for Discussing Imagery through modeling and praise. Finally, be sure to encourage accountable talk by asking students to cite evidence in the text for each claim. This is especially useful for ELLs.

Lesson Step 4.3: Preparing a Recitation

1. In this culminating performance activity, students select a poem from the Poetry Out Loud website or another reputable source and prepare a recitation of it. To help them make the transition from group performance activities to individual recitations, provide students with the handout Getting Ready to Recite (handout 4.A in the appendix) and review it with them.

2. Have students view a model recitation of "Facing It" and a few other poems and discuss the features of a recitation.

3. After students select a poem, provide time for students to practice their close reading strategies and submit illustrations or written work as they prepare performances.

4. As they begin memorizing, have students rewrite the poem on their own sheet of paper as a series of sentences, and again as a series of lines. Not only is it helpful in the memorization process, but the process helps readers notice aspects of language that would otherwise go unnoticed. It is also a great preview of the lessons on line breaks and sentence features in the other chapters. Finally, have students try to label the tone of the speaker's voice as it changes from one line or phrase to the next. For more information on this process, see the "Tone Map" assignment on the Poetry Out Loud website.

5. Build in a small group performance workshop, so students have the opportunity to practice and receive feedback from a small group of trusted peers before the final performance, which you might evaluate using the rubric available on the Poetry Out Loud website or another performance rubric.

6. Make performances something of an event. Whether it is a class competition or a showcase, this is the culmination of a lot of improvisational training, trust building, and good reading, so it is something to celebrate. Create or move to a special performance space and invite an audience (other teachers, classes, parents, community members, etc.). Students may even videotape performances to share with a larger audience using websites like www.schooltube.com.

More Poems for Practice

Using the same close reading techniques they have learned in previous lessons, students can explore other poems to determine the emotional curve of a poem of place. "Where I'm From" by George Ella Lyon (widely accessible), "Chicago" by Carl Sandburg (more challenging), and "London" by William Blake (difficult) lend themselves easily to these explorations. Students of all levels can be assessed using the recitation technique, though the preparation process, written pre-recitation products, and evaluation of these students may vary.

More Close Reading, Performance, and Powerful Writing Ideas

Close Reading

Have students complete the following claim statement and support it using evidence from the text: "In his or her poem "_____," the poet _____ uses images of _____ in his or her exploration of _____, which, as the images suggest, is/was a _____ topic/experience." (Sample: In his poem "Facing It" the poet Yusef Komunyakaa uses images of nature, monuments, and other mourners to represent his memories of the Vietnam War, which is a haunting experience for him.)

Performance

Students can create video montages with voiceovers of "Facing It."

Artful Writing

Students may write a brief vignette (not necessarily a poem) about a visit to a memorial or monument or another place that is a sacred reminder of someone who has passed on.

Additional Resources for Chapter 2

Poems, Poets, Poetry

"Still I Rise" by Maya Angelou

- Video made with images and Angelou's own reading http://www.redroom.com/video/still-i-rise
- Video of Angelou reading the poem http://www.youtube.com/watch?v=JqOqo50LSZ0&feature=related

"Facing It" by Yusef Komunyakaa

- An audio clip of the poem. http://www.poetryfoundation.org/journal/audioitem.html?id=594

- *Pleasure Dome: New and Collected Poems* by Yusef Komunyakaa (Middleton: Wesleyan UP, 2001).

"To His Coy Mistress" by Andrew Marvel

- Eleven audio recordings of the poem http://www.archive.org/details/To_His_Coy_Mistress
- Another reading of the poem http://ecaudio.umwblogs.org/marvell-to-his-coy-mistress-read-by-meredith-nowlin/

"I Go Back to May 1937" by Sharon Olds

- A video of the poem read by the poet http://www.poetry-foundation.org/journal/videoitem.html?id=26

Other Reliable Sources of Texts

- www.poetryfoundation.org
- www.poets.org
- www.bartleby.com

Definitions/Words/Etymology

- www.poetryfoundation.org (Literary Glossary)
- www.etymonline.com (Etymology)
- www.askoxford.com (Dictionary)

Audiovisual Resources

- Vietnam Memorial: http://www.greatbuildings.com/cgi-bin/gbi.cgi/Vietnam_Veterans_Memorial.html/cid_2877635.jpg.
- Google Images has just about everything from portraits of poets to images of details from the poems, and even examples of tableau vivant.
- The Poet Speaks of Art (Poems inspired by famous paintings): http://www.english.emory.edu/classes/paintings&poems/titlepage.html
- YouTube has some great resources for theater games and examples of tableau vivant as it is woven into theatrical performances, including those of Lookingglass Theatre, which develops many of its productions through its work with physicalizing longer canonical texts, a process similar to the one I advocate throughout lessons with brief lyrics. Along with Jeff Wilhelm, Lookingglass Theatre has been my greatest resource.

Other Resources

- "The Rhetorical Situation," *Purdue OWL*, Purdue University Online Writing Lab, http://owl.english.purdue.edu/owl/resource/625/01/. A number of wonderful resources for students and teachers are available at www.ReadWriteThink.org, including rubrics for evaluating everything from small group discussions to academic essays, comic books, and performances. The comic creator, digital scrapbook, timeline, and other interactive tools for students can help teachers facilitate visualization activities.

Professional Development Resources

- As I have developed a repertoire of theater techniques, I have relied heavily on the workshops facilitated by members of the Lookingglass Theatre Company and the scholar/author Jeffery D. Wilhelm, especially his books *Action Strategies for Deepening Comprehension* and *Reading Is Seeing*.

- To build professional fluency in talking about imagery and figurative language, see Helen Vendler's *Poems, Poets, Poetry* anthology (especially her "Describing Poems" chapter) and Edward Hirsch's article "The Poet Is a Nightingale," available online at the Poetry Foundation website, http://www.poetryfoundation.org/.

- For literary terms, I have relied heavily on M. H. Abrams, *A Glossary of Literary Terms*. It has great examples and nuanced explanations.

3 Teaching Close Reading and Powerful Writing through Imitation

Poems as Models for Imitation

The lessons in this chapter present students with a brief introduction to some of the forms and techniques of traditional poets. Applying the close reading and performance / recitation techniques developed in the second chapter of this book, students will read and perform models of the free verse, hymn, and sonnet forms. After each close reading and performance activity, students will explore one or two formal poetic techniques ranging from line break to sonic patterning in their own imitative works. Through these exercises, students will gain a deeper awareness of the impact of form on meaning and will gain additional practice in using genre awareness to tackle difficult texts. Students will then workshop each of their original works using the Workshop Templates.

The Workshop Templates (handout 5.E in the appendix) allows students to make claims about the choices their peers make and to practice using the language of literature to describe text. The template focuses student attention on describing the texts their peers created before jumping to suggested revisions or simply pointing out conventional errors. Building on the Think-Aloud Prompts from the previous chapter and More Think-Aloud Prompts from this chapter (handout 5.B in the appendix), the Workshop Templates also act as the next step in students' introduction to making formal academic claims about texts, while simultaneously training students for workshops in academic writing.

Lesson 5: Structural Devices in Free Verse

Teacher-to-Teacher Note. This is the first of several model lessons on teaching poetic structures and forms through imitation. While this first poem is longer and rich with allusions that might be challenging for some students, there is a "common sense" appeal that makes this piece popular with diverse populations of students. This appeal also makes it work well in performance. The list poem exercise in the creative writing prompt is a great first assignment for a creative writing unit as well. Creating a list is something even the most struggling, novice, or bashful writer can easily do. Adding the structure of repetition and strategic line break quickly produces poetic effects, a pleasure for any beginning writer. Before sharing the poem, distribute and review Key Literary Terms for Discussing Poetic Forms and Techniques and More Think-Aloud Prompts (handouts 5.A and 5.B in the appendix). For the first lesson, students will focus on the terms *verse*, *free verse*, *enjambment*, and *allusion*. For reliable sources of the text, see the sources in "Additional Resources for Chapter 3" at the end of this chapter.

Lesson Step 5.1: Introducing Free Verse with "I Am Waiting" by Lawrence Ferlinghetti

1. *Frontloading Knowledge Option:* Like previous lessons, the over-arching objective of this lesson is to make authorial choice more obvious to students by giving them opportunities to explore, describe, and imitate. To begin, show students the clip of *Star Wars Episode V: The Empire Strikes Back* in which Darth Vader reveals that he is Luke Skywalker's father. Then show students the clip of *Toy Story 2*, where Zurg reveals that he is Buzz Lightyear's father. Ask, "Why is the *Toy Story* scene so funny?" Lead a discussion with students noting that by playing with an audience's knowledge of genre and their specific knowledge of *Star Wars*, the *Toy Story 2* creators were playing with an allusion for humorous effect. This skilled choice is what makes the audience laugh. Tell students that they will be focused more and more on finding, describing, and making skilled authorial choices like these.

2. *Additional Frontloading Knowledge Option*: In addition to Woodrow Wilson's 1917 declaration of war, Ferlinghetti uses other biblical, mythical, literary, and historical allusions (references to a well-known person, place, event, or text). If you and your students aren't sure where they are, begin by looking for words and phrases that are capitalized, such as "Age of Anxiety," "Second Coming," and "Grapes of Wrath." If the poet's use of more difficult allusions presents a huge stumbling block for some of your students, don't worry. You can easily enjoy the poem on other levels without the research. However, since we lucky twenty-first-century readers can use an Internet search engine to find out what they reference, discovering allusions in chunks of the poem is a wonderful prereading project for students if time allows. Creating a hypertext edition of the poem by creating a link to information on each allusion is equally worthwhile as a culminating task, especially if you ask students to write reflections about the impact of the choices on the overall meaning of the poem.

3. Create placards with these questions on them and hand them to individual and small groups of students to perform: What are

YOU waiting for? What are you WAITING for? WHAT are you waiting FOR? Tell performers to ham up the word that appears in all caps as they ask the question written on the placard. Make sure every student performs the vocal task and reflects on the changing question in varying intonations. In the debrief, point out that playing with possible *stress* variations in the key line of the poem, "i am WAITing," "I am waiting," and "i AM waiting," students consider how tone can also be affected by *duration, volume,* and *pitch*. Dragging out a syllable can change this statement to mean anything from *"you're taking too long"* to *"I am hopeful."* This is a poem in which students can really play with the interpretive powers of their own voices, a wonderful reading strategy to employ with poetry.

4. In a large group debrief, challenge students to discuss how the meaning and tone of the utterance changes as the speakers intone it differently. Explain that this repetition, which exploits the multiplicity of meanings, is one of the structural devices Ferlinghetti uses in this free verse masterpiece. Free verse is a poetry form that is free of restrictions in terms of particular metric patterns, rhyme schemes, or other formal rules; nevertheless, while a less rigid form than others, free verse is a form. Using strategic line break, repetition, and other structural moves, poets like Ferlinghetti give poems a form of their own.

5. Before having students explore repetition, allusion, and line break throughout the poem, show them through a close reading of a few examples how the poet breaks the lines, repeatedly toying with allusions to well-known sound bites of American speech.

Here is how I model the close reading:

> Consider these lines: "and I am waiting for the war to be fought / which will make the world safe." <u>This is an allusion because it is almost a quote from</u> President Wilson's declaration of war against Germany in 1917, in which he declared, "The world must be made safe for democracy."

Then I ask students to consider how these lines sound when they are followed by "for Anarchy." (You may need to define the term, which means absence of government.) If they are familiar with the term *anarchy*, students will immediately see that the addition of "for Anarchy" after the line break adds a devilishly ironic twist to the statement.

> Now instead of seeing war as a strategy for peace, as Wilson did, the speaker suggests that we'd all be better off without governments that are at war with each other. The line break allows us to read the sentence in two completely different ways, and these incongruous views of government make it funny. The line break delays his punch line just enough so that the tone changes almost covertly from serious and patriotic to cleverly rebellious (just like Zurg!).

6. Explain that one of the great lessons to learn from this poem is how to handle a line break. This text is chock full of enjambment—when the unit of thought runs over the line break or verse break. Enjambment allows a thought within a sentence to make sense in a new way if the reader stops at the end of the line rather than the end of the sentence. Often, the poem's humor relies upon the fact that stopping at the end of the line gives the reader a different, more conventional sense of the text than it gives when it is read as part of the sentence, which often imparts a new, humorous take on a cliché.

7. Allowing students to explore the doubleness of this technique requires experimentation. Perform a shared think-aloud by having students take a close look at the first stanza of the poem. The first thirteen lines of the poem sound at times like an everyday "Joe" lamenting the unfulfilled promises of the American dream—a conventional higher ideal. By line 14 though, the poem takes a twist, and the speaker unleashes a radical antigovernment, anarchist philosophy. Have students walk through this script and see this "subscriber-to-higher-ideal/rascally-cynic" pattern repeated over and over again. Have them look for the same pattern in the next stanza. For example, the second stanza quickly juxtaposes the Christian ideal of the Second Coming with the shallowest brand of televangelism.

8. Give students a chance to use their own eyes and ears to enjoy the humor of the repetition and the line breaks, especially when they are used with familiar idioms and allusions. Have students work in three small groups. Assign each group a stanza and have them select a small chunk of text (ten lines or so) and prepare to physicalize the text in an ad hoc performance. Give them a few minutes to prepare a reading that involves all the members of the group, using various combinations of voices. ELLs may need additional assistance with idioms.

9. Bring the large group back together and have students share possible claims about the gist of the poem. As students begin constructing a summary, refer to the SOAPSTone display to have them make more precise claims about the rhetorical situation.

Lesson Step 5.2 (Optional): Getting Ready to Recite "I Am Waiting"

Teacher-to-Teacher Note. Reciting this poem individually is a huge undertaking, but preparing a recitation of even a segment of the poem is well worth the experience for a serious student of poetry and perhaps even for the budding comic. You may choose to capitalize on the group performance strategies of earlier lessons. If recitation is the chosen route, use the following recitation guide in conjunction with the recitation assignment in Chapter 2, lesson 4 to coach students through the process.

1. Share and review the Getting Ready to Recite: "I Am Waiting" student handout (5.C in the appendix).

2. After students share performances of the piece, debrief the effect of preparing for performance on their understanding of the poem. This metacognitive reflection is essential in developing an enduring sense that reading aloud to one's self and others can be a helpful way of tackling tough texts.

Lesson Step 5.3: Exploring Free Verse through Imitation

Teacher-to-Teacher Note. The "I Am Waiting" creative writing prompt works well as a springboard for a collaborative poem, a set of original poems for performance, or just a good old-fashioned individual poetry-writing assignment. In my experience, the assignment is as engaging as the original poem and appeals to even the most reluctant student, because asking students to create a list, as opposed to a poem, makes it easy to get started.

1. Remind students of their previous discussions about the selection and arrangement of images. On their next stop in the 360-degree tour, they are stepping into the writing of a poem to see, firsthand, how authors shape meaning purposefully by making choices.

2. To increase the chances of students writing something vivid, start by ruling out the use of emotion labels (love, anger, sadness, depression, hurt, happiness, excitement, etc., are off limits). Tell students they must instead describe these emotions in physical terms only. Here are a few examples I use: Instead of *I felt mad*, write, *I clenched my teeth*. Instead of *I was embarrassed*, use *the heat of shame reddened my face*.

3. Distribute Artful Writing: Composing Free Verse (handout 5.D) and have students complete the "Image Generator" portion in class, writing as many images as they can in a given time (at least fifteen minutes).

4. Ask students to revise their work at home, reconsidering word choice and consciously selecting and arranging the images that will end up in the complete draft.

Lesson Step 5.4: Facilitating Peer Workshops with the Workshop Templates

Teacher-to-Teacher Note. Templates throughout the 360-degree tour reinforce the idea that texts (students' own texts, their peers' texts, and published texts) are products of authorial choice. Learning to examine text through this lens helps students become more astute describers of text for claim-making purposes. Learning to see and describe various aspects of text makes students more capable as readers of imaginative and academic writing and more conscious editors of their own work and that of their peers because they are prompted to see readings as pieces of writing and products of both author choice and reader experience.

The Workshop Templates (see handout 5.E in the appendix) are designed to help students describe first, suggest later. This allows the reviewer to honor peer work with sophisticated descriptive claims while practicing evidence-based claim making, an essential academic skill. Through this process, students learn to speak to each other respectfully and, in many ways, more usefully about revision because they discuss how input from the text (author's choice) connects to their own experience as readers, the associated meanings.

Otherwise known as inferences, *associated meanings* can be very specific personal experiences or more generic ideas, such as the pictures of concrete images that come to mind. They can also be meanings we associate with the text because we've seen them before as readers or movie watchers, and so forth. The story of a princess falling in love with a prince or a boy setting off on a long journey that becomes an adventure ending in manhood are typical master narratives. A master narrative with which we may have personal or cultural experience then becomes a lens through which we see other texts. Finally, there are very specific reading experiences, such as reading other texts from the same genre (other sonnets), the traditional uses of a particular metaphor (tropes such as water as a symbol of cleansing), or seeing certain specialized terms from a particular discourse community ("waiting for my case to come up" is a phrase from the criminal justice discourse community).

The template prompts students to spell out those connections, so others can see how the author's choice led to the reader's claim. This, in my experience, is one of the biggest teaching challenges in all of literature! (Later, the Describing Text Templates in the academic writing sequence will capitalize on student practice with the Workshop Templates. For more on the continuity between templates, see Chapter 1, which describes the 360-degree approach and the rationale behind the writers workshop.)

1. Have students exchange papers and complete the workshop templates. Students must write at least two Description Claims and two Suggestion Claims. Be sure students feel free to add additional comments as well and write as much as possible on the text.

2. Have students share feedback with each other in class. The writers should remain silent until the reviewers have shared their feedback. Then the writers can clarify their understanding of the reviewers' comments and talk about their original intentions.

3. As you circulate, be sure to praise students for the use of key terms.

4. Highlight a few writers for a whole group workshop during the second half of each session. Not only is this useful for the writer, who will hear more feedback and will hear your comments as well; but it is an essential part of developing the collaborative culture that will be so valuable for improving peer reviewer skills and making all students feel comfortable making claims about text.

More Poems for Practice

"Beautiful Black Men" by Nikki Giovanni (widely accessible for most high school students), "I Hear America Singing" by Walt Whitman, the father of American free verse (more challenging), "A Supermarket in California" by Allen Ginsberg—a great pairing for the Whitman piece (still more difficult than the Whitman piece for most high school students). Each is rich with opportunities to examine repetition, the free verse form, and the techniques of allusion and strategic line break. To assess students at lower levels of readiness, have them select a free verse poem and work in pairs or small groups using strategies from the previous lessons to determine the answers to SOAPSTone questions. Have students who are on level read aloud one of the poems above and annotate it, noting an author's use of repetition, strategic line break, or allusion. Have advanced students extend the annotation by writing about the purpose or effect of particular formal choice (line break, allusion, repetition) and how it relates to the meaning of the poem. Instruct students to use the Description Template from the workshop handout to generate sentences.

More Close Reading, Performance, and Powerful Writing Ideas

Close Reading

Have students complete the following template: "In the poem, Ferlinghetti makes many arguments about what it is like to live in the modern world, including the argument that _____." Have students support the claim with specific references to the text, using the Describing Text Claim Template used in 5.E to develop supporting sentences.

Performance

Researching the allusions in this piece is an education in itself. Giving the students an opportunity to link this text to other texts (via hyperlink or annotated script) as a dramaturge in a professional theater will lead them through an exciting literary and historical journey that will make the intricacies of this poem's architecture more visible. Dramaturges might then collaborate with a director, actors, and set designers to produce a performance piece, selecting a set design, costumes, props, and so forth for a formal performance. Having multiple classes each perform a longer poem on the modern American experience would make a wonderful end-of-semester show.

Artful Writing

This makes a wonderful starting point for a group performance piece. Students can use pieces of their original wish lists in concert with "I Am Waiting" in a collaborative poem for publishing or performance.

Lesson 6: Rhythm in a Hymn

Teacher-to-Teacher Note. In this lesson, students will explore one poet's use of the hymn as a formal poetic structure and as a genre with a particular history that informs a reader's interpretation of all texts in the form. Students will practice looking for patterns and variations in rhythm within this structure, learning the basic skills for identifying other metrical patterns along the way. Using one of Emily Dickinson's early definition poems as a template, students will also have the opportunity to try their hand at writing a poem that follows particular rhythm patterns. As students craft their poems, they will gain introductory knowledge of the art of prosody. For reliable sources of the text, see "Additional Resources for Chapter 3" at the end of the chapter. As always, encourage students to use their Key Terms (handouts 1.B and 5.A) and their Think-Aloud Prompts (handouts 1.C and 5.B).

Lesson Step 6.1: Introducing Rhythm through Emily Dickinson's "'Hope' is the thing with feathers"

1. *Frontloading Knowledge Option:* Ask students to complete a quick-write of a time when they really hoped for something that was improbable. Winning the lotto is a good example of something improbable for which a lot of people have hoped hard, though there is little chance of success. Have them pair and share their examples, and then discuss the question, "what were the plusses and minuses of having hope in that situation?" Then in a large group discussion of the concept, brainstorm answers to the following questions about defining aspects of hope: What is hope's function or purpose? What is the same or the opposite of hope? What are the causes and effects of hope? Tell students they will be studying one poet's definition of hope in their next close reading.

2. Introduce students to the idea that more contemporary forms, such as free verse, are responses to older forms in a great, ongoing conversation between the poets of the ages. Poets continue to contribute innovative bodies of work to the long tradition of formal poetry by introducing new subjects and playing with traditional structures. Let them know that in addition to learning about rhythm and meter, the building blocks of all metrical verse, they will be learning about the hymn as a poetic form.

3. Before having students explore the poem—Emily Dickinson's "'Hope' is the thing with feathers"—I talk a little about the anxiety students might be feeling. For some students, this will be an introduction to the notion of formal rhythm and meter, but others may express apprehension based on some earlier introduction to it. Many students fear the difficulty of this aspect of poetry, which is often presented using jargon or impenetrable language. I tell my students that learning about rhythm in poetry intimidates many readers of poetry, including teachers. The language that experts use to discuss rhythm often seems not only inscrutable but also an almost purposefully highfalutin way of keeping poetry at a safe distance from the rest of us. Assure students that we can still enjoy poetry without these terms, but explain that noticing the way in which writers manipulate this formal element can reveal another source of delight for readers and provide a wonderful tool for aspiring writers.

    Dickinson's poem offers us a glimpse of how a simple variation in a pattern of rhythm can be used to draw readers to a new entrance into the poem. Let students know that for this lesson—but not always—they will take a look at the rhythm before they delve into a close reading. Advise them that this exercise is easier to do if they don't think too much about the meaning of words and concentrate instead on the sounds of the poem.

4. Point out that the key to determining meter is looking for patterns of stressed and unstressed syllables. Tell them that they should forget about the terms and listen for a pattern. They will simply be using their voices and their hands to determine the pattern of stressed and unstressed syllables. The number of beats is the number of stressed syllables, otherwise known as beats in each line. Distribute the poem.

5. Have students hum the poem several times out loud. As they hum, have them clap along to determine the total number of syllables in each line. Remind them that they were perfectly capable of doing such work when they were in kindergarten, so they should not be afraid to do it now.

    In a second round of humming and clapping, have students determine the pattern of beats (stressed syllables) in each line. Tell them to clap along now as if they were clapping to a song, not clapping on every syllable, just clapping to the rhythm. You might demonstrate this with a nursery song such as Miss Mary Mack: Miss (clap) Mary Mack (clap) Mack (clap) Mack (clap). There are four beats. Students will see that there are a certain number of beats in each line if they allow themselves to hear the music of the lines, rather than thinking about the meaning of words and sentences. The more they separate the meaning of the words from the sound of the line, the clearer the patterns will become. The pattern of beats will begin to emerge in rote repetition, so insist on a number of run-throughs.

Stop and ask everyone to raise their hand if they think they have detected a pattern. If a majority of students raise their hands, ask the students who are having trouble getting it to try to describe their problem. This will open up opportunities to respond to questions about what constitutes a stress. Ask students to think back to the "I Am Waiting" exercise and to remember that stress can come in many forms (duration, pitch, or volume) and sound different in each pair of syllables. Tell them the focus is on the pattern of stresses. Then ask the whole group to hum their performance (humming and clapping) for the class, demonstrating that the words of the poem may sound different, but that there is an underlying pattern to the stressed beats.

6. To illustrate the pattern visually, project the text. At the end of each line, record student findings about the number of syllables. Next, ask students to identify stresses and represent them visually by marking each stressed syllable using the symbol we use in formal scansion (´). Next, mark the unstressed syllables (˘). The poem's overall pattern is eight-syllable lines alternating with six-syllable lines. Point out that *almost* without exception, the lines have a pattern of unstressed then stressed syllables. Then mark the divisions between syllables (/) to indicate pairs. Project the word *Iamb* along with its definition—a two-syllable foot made up of an unstressed syllable followed by a stressed syllable. Tell students that this is the name given to this combination of syllables, the most common poetic foot in the English language. Add that we name a poem's formal meter by the kind of foot (in this case iambic) and the number of feet in the line (in this case *tetrameter* for four feet and *trimeter* for three feet). Joseph Powell and Mark Halperin's *Accent on Meter* and Robert Pinsky's *The Sounds of Poetry* are excellent sources for more detailed explanations of rhythm and scansion. For now, though, it is only necessary to know about iambs. Tell them that we can describe a poem's meter by the general pattern, even when there are exceptions to the pattern.

7. I wrap up the rhythm section of this discussion by alerting students to the fact that the form Dickinson chose to use was the same as that of a traditional hymn, which is a religious song of praise, usually sung. It was a popular form in Dickinson's time. I share this additional background information about her as well:

Emily Dickinson was a reclusive woman who lived in Amherst, Massachusetts, and wrote an enormous collection of mostly unpublished poems during the middle part of the nineteenth century. While she published only eleven poems in her own lifetime, today she is considered one of the greatest poets in the English language. This is one of her early definition poems.

8. Have students work in small groups, using their close reading/visualization magic to determine the antecedent scenario, identify the rhetorical situation (SOAPSTone), divide the poem into parts, and paraphrase it. Provide access to print or online dictionaries so students can pay close attention to word choice. Mention that the Dickinsons knew the Websters, the dictionary-writing family, and that their dictionary was an important source for her work.

   In a large group debrief, have several groups share their findings until the whole class has the gist of the poem.

9. Ask students, why might she have selected this traditional, religious form, the hymnal structure, to explore the idea of hope? Your discussion may lead to the connection between the form, traditionally used in religious contexts, and the role of hope in certain theologies. You might also point out the comforting chant-like qualities of the form, which compliment the ideas she discusses. Bring the discussion back to the form, and return to the idea that form is connected to meaning, highlighting that the sound of a poem echoes its sense of comfort and hope. In other words, the manner in which a poet writes has something to do with the matter.

10. For the final leg of this discussion, I return to the role of rhythm patterns and variations in the meaning of a poem. I remind students that there is only one exception to the eight/six syllable pattern (in the first word of the poem) and ask them to hypothesize about Dickinson's choice. Encourage students to make claims describing the piece in terms of authorial choice. To do this, encourage students to use the language provided in the Description Template on the Workshop Templates handout.

11. Students immediately point out that it is the most important word and that it is in the first line. I ask them to consider which syllable is missing (the first unstressed syllable of the first iamb) and ask why that might be the case. After having students share observations about other differences they find in the first line, such as quotes around the first word, I suggest that noticing slight variations in a pattern is essential to being a close reader and that variations are not accidents but meaningful choices that poets make.

12. After having spent time with some of the key images and techniques (the bird-like personification of hope, storms, the hymn, etc.) ask students to consider Dickinson's argument. In other

words, how she might have answered the prereading questions about hope (Function/purpose, opposite/same as, and cause/effect)? What claims does she make about the nature of hope? How do her choices (images, the hymn/religious form, speaker point of view, appeals to ethos, pathos, and logos, etc.) help her make that argument? Give students a chance to jot down their own answers then share with their groups.

After a robust discussion where students make claims about the poem's meaning, remind them that all poems are arguments, just like love songs. Poets make arguments about the nature of being human and all sorts of other things using the tools of their trade!

13. As the discussion closes, I assure students that they will have plenty of time to practice determining rhythm and to become fluent in talking about rhythm's relationship to meaning as they explore more formal poems. They will also have much more practice at looking for patterns and variations in patterns as well.

Lesson Step 6.2: Getting Ready to Recite "'Hope' is the thing with feathers"

1. Have students prepare recitations of this poem using Getting Ready to Recite (the student handout 6.A provided in the appendix). Even many young students are able to master a performance of this piece, and, I have to say, it is such a nice piece to have in one's repertoire of memorized poems. Preparing this piece for recitation is also a great way for students to understand the variations within metered verse. A recitation that demonstrates true understanding does not sound singsongy, like the mechanical definition of iambic pentameter might suggest. When students reunite the sounds of the words and sentences with their meanings, they will see that one accented or stressed syllable (one beat) in a line might sound very different from another accented syllable, yet in terms of describing the meter of a poem, these variations don't matter. *When describing meter, the pattern of unstressed and stressed syllables is all that matters, but in recitation the sound of the sentence is what matters.*

2. After sharing recitations, have students discuss their final interpretations based on the question, "To whom does the speaker speak and why?" Also ask, "What did this lesson teach you about the nature of rhythm as a technical craft? As a guide to performance?" Have students quick-write their answers separately before the large group discussion.

Lesson Step 6.3: Exploring the Hymn through Imitation

Teacher-to-Teacher Note. Dickinson's first line is a template for a metaphor, so filling in her template is one way to get students exploring writer's craft by trying it out. Don't forget, imitation is an important part of the 360-degree approach and a load of fun. I have yet to meet a student who could not name an emotion, so the challenge is getting to the next step, comparing that internal feeling to something that the rest of the world can experience through their senses. In my experience, students do rise to the challenge and enjoy the fact that the template has helped them to create poetry, or something akin to it, almost instantly. Once they have generated the initial material, they can really begin tinkering with word choice, imagery, and even the idea of iambs—a good place to start learning about the intricacies of rhythm-consciousness.

1. Remind students that first and foremost they must be vivid! The words human beings use to describe our concrete world may be different, but the sensory experiences of images are common. For example, while we might all understand what it feels like when the wind blows, each of us connects the sensory experience with unique feelings that can then be understood by others.

2. Provide students with the assignment Artful Writing: Attending to Rhythm (see the student handout 6.B in the appendix) and review it. Then provide class time for initial drafting. Again, for those who hesitate to write in class, suggest that there is absolutely no pressure to write a poem, only to try to find an image that conveys a feeling. After they get something down, you can help them develop their piece with more details.

3. Have students complete drafts at home and gather ideas for further revision in small group and large group workshops using the Workshop Templates (handout 5.E) and accompanying steps found in lesson step 5.4.

4. These definition poems make wonderful additions to the walls of a school. A set of student-made posters is perfect for a class display, which can line a wall in a hallway, a library, or a classroom.

More Poems for Practice

"It Couldn't Be Done" by Edgar Albert Guest (widely accessible), "Analysis of Baseball" by May Swenson (widely accessible), and "Poems Are Hard to Read" by William Matthews (challenging) offer really great examples of how looking for repetition and variation in rhythm pays off in close reading. To assess students at lower levels of readiness, have them take the Guest or Swenson poem and practice the hum/clap technique independently. Have them mark the number of beats in each line for a minimum of four lines. For an additional challenge, have them divide the iambs. On-level students might scan the entire poem and write a brief description of the metrical pattern at work in the poem. They can also add their comments about the reasons why Guest or Swenson may have elected to use this metrical pattern to discuss the ideas presented in the poem. Advanced students can try their hand at more advanced manipulations of rhythm by scanning the Matthews poem and discussing the connection between images and rhythm patterns. Eric Murphy Selinger at DePaul University introduced me to this activity. It is a wonderful illustration of how a poet manipulates rhythm to reflect meaning!

More Close Reading, Performance, and Powerful Writing Ideas

Close Reading

Have students read Dickinson's other definition poems, particularly those that define hope in different ways. Have them compare and contrast her personification of hope in each; then students should fill out the following claim template and support it in a paragraph using details from the text. Emily Dickinson characterizes hope as _____, _____, _____ in three different definition poems, arguing that she believed hope to be _____ and _____, yet _____.

Performance

A group performance of original and published poems around a particular theme could be a wonderful opportunity for students to play with rhythm, using performance styles ranging from traditional recitations to slam-style performance pieces. Like contemporary performance poetry, Dickinson's poem plays upon the pleasures of steady rhythm patterns. For examples of slam performances, see *Slam Nation* and HBO's *Def Poetry*. Be sure to preview them, as not all of the content is suitable for educational purposes. Have students create a sound track for these poems using only their bodies and the floor to highlight rhythm patterns.

Artful Writing

The definition poem format works well over and over again. Dickinson wrote quite a few, several of which defined and redefined the same concepts. Students may choose to toy with this format using different concepts and using some of Dickinson's other definition poems as springboards or examples.

Lesson 7: Quatrains and Couplets in Sonnet Arguments

Teacher-to-Teacher Note. You might be wondering why I don't use Shakespeare to introduce the Shakespearean sonnet. First, my students have always found Claude McKay's "If We Must Die" engaging, powerful, and even inspirational. Some have heard it quoted before and quickly understand its historical significance. For many students, the language is also more accessible than Shakespeare's, yet the elevated, sometimes archaic diction acts as a good introduction to the Bard's language, which I do ask them to study later. Finally, in the context of introducing imitation as an entrée to more artful writing, I think it is appropriate to show that writing in a revered form is a challenge great poets relish, not just an English teacher's assignment. McKay's poem is a good example of a poet capitalizing on the history of a form, knowing that his audience's familiarity with the revered European genre will cast his response to atrocities against twentieth-century African Americans in a different light.

You may also note that this lesson's focus is on argument, not on the typically highlighted elements of the form (rhythm and rhyme), but rather on the development of the images and ideas within the argument-driven sonnet structure. I do this because having students consider the substantive parts of a sonnet, rather than simply the rhythm and rhyme formula, moves them into a whole different critical stance in reading literary texts and in their thinking about their own work as sonneteers. The result is better close reading and more sophisticated understandings of what it takes to write a good sonnet. As a creative writing teacher, I have also found that a focus on vivid imagery and argument over formal techniques always yields better imitations of the form.

Starting with the question, "How do poets use quatrains and couplets within a sonnet to develop and build arguments?" students will apply the close reading and recitation strategies from this lesson, as well as earlier lessons, to gain a deeper understanding of the form of sonnets. Using the very fun, imitative, artful writing exercise included, students will then have an opportunity to gain an even more intimate understanding of the form by looking at it from the inside, through the eyes of a writer. For reliable sources of the text, see "Additional Resources for Chapter 3" at the end of the chapter.

Lesson Step 7.1: Introducing the Shakespearean Sonnet with "If We Must Die" by Claude McKay

1. *Frontloading Knowledge Option:* Have students perform a quick-write in response to the following questions: "Have you ever been in a situation in which you had to respond to an injustice but felt powerless (a false accusation, an unjust punishment, bullying, or alienation by a peer group, etc.)? How did you respond? What were the consequences of choosing that response? What factors

shaped your choice? What were other possible choices and potential consequences?" Then, have students pair up and discuss the outcomes of their choices, using the question, "Looking back, do you feel you made the right decision or do you wish you had acted differently?" Assure students that they need not share the details of the situation with anyone, and they can therefore talk in general terms. Remind them also of their rights and responsibilities as members of a supportive learning community and your own obligations as a professional. Next, facilitate a large group debrief based on the question, "What kinds of responses are available to us in the face of injustice?" After the discussion, let students know that they will be reading a poem that was one poet's response to the injustices of Red Summer, a term used to describe the race riots of 1919. Share a brief summary of this historical period. Additional resources from PBS's Jim Crow Stories can be found at http://www.pbs.org/wnet/jimcrow/stories_events_red.html. For additional background information, you will find these search terms useful: Festus Claudius McKay, Harlem Renaissance, Sonnet, Volta, 1919 Race Riots, Red Summer, and Red Scare.

2. Share a little background about the poet and the form: Claude McKay was a poet whose works are associated with the literary period known as the Harlem Renaissance, a twentieth-century African American literature and arts movement. While his work reflects the African heritage of his birthplace, Jamaica, much of his literary style echoes the work of European writers as well. In this well-known piece, McKay adapts the conventions of the English or Shakespearean sonnet, a form named after one of its greatest practitioners, William Shakespeare. Like Shakespeare's sonnets, which form compact arguments about various romantic and intellectual topics, McKay's piece argues for resistance in the face of oppression.

3. Have students read the poem aloud several times, individually or in small groups. Have them exaggerate the dramatic rise and fall in the speaker's voice. As they practice reading aloud, have them also listen to the changes in the pace of the poem, making notes about where the drama seems to intensify and where it slows down. Even without a close reading, the title, along with McKay's use of apostrophes and exclamation points, indicates the dramatic nature of this sonnet, which students quickly begin to hear more keenly through this read-aloud technique.

4. After performing the read-aloud, have students practice visualizing images by illustrating and thinking aloud about the poem using the techniques from the previous chapter and additional strategies introduced earlier in this chapter.

5. Open a large group discussion of the gist of the poem by asking, "Even if we didn't know when this poem was written or by

whom, what do we know about the antecedent scenario?" Have students share possible claims to answer SOAPSTone questions. Encourage students to practice stating their claims carefully, describing the text in terms of authorial choice. If students still struggle with formulating claims about author's craft, encourage them to use the language provided in the Description Template found on the Workshop Templates handout. Have them modify it to say, "When the speaker in McKay's poem said _____ it made me think _____, because when most people think of _____, they think _____."

6. After getting the gist of the poem, ask students to work in small groups to divide the poem into parts, discussing the characteristics that make one part distinct from another. Astute readers will immediately point to rhyme schemes, repeated sentence starters, various commands that separate parts, and so forth. Most students can usually find three major breaks (the quatrains). In my experience, they often lump the final couplet (the volta) with the third quatrain.

   Again, take the time to praise students for using Key Literary Terms and the Workshop Templates or Describing Text Templates (handout 9.D). I can't say enough about the importance of this kind of praise in good modeling.

7. After students have had a chance to use their own eyes and ears to find the "parts" of the text, let them know that these parts reflect adherence to a particular form. These are the features as I describe them:

   > More frequently referred to as the Shakespearean sonnet, the fourteen-line poems called English sonnets usually have an abab cdcd efef gg rhyme scheme, made up of three quatrains—four line stanzas—and a couplet—a two-line stanza at the end called the *volta*.

   If necessary bring them back to the text to show them how to determine the rhyme scheme. I explain it this way.

   > Assign the letter *a* to the first line of the poem. Assign the same letter to each line that rhymes with it. Assign the letter *b* to the first line that doesn't rhyme with the *a* lines. Then assign the letter *b* to every line that rhymes with it. Use the next letter of the alphabet for each new rhyme. As you read the poem aloud, note how the rhyme scheme offers a way of dividing the poem into four parts: abab, cdcd, efef, and gg.

   You can also mention that Shakespeare's sonnets are written in a particular meter, iambic pentameter, which is usually ten syllables, following an unstressed/stressed pattern.

   In addition to sharing these characteristics, I like Ron Padgett's simple idea that a sonnet is a fourteen-line poem that "involves a certain way of thinking: the setting up or development of a thought or idea which is brought to a conclusion by the end of the poem" (Padgett 178). For close reading purposes, this is the most important part of the sonnet definition thus far.

8. In small groups, have students explore the poem more closely now, with the formal features in mind. The following questions are useful, but a generic focus on what is repeated and what is different in each part of the poem is enough for many students to discover the impact of the artist's choices.

   ■ Consider the change in imagery that occurs between the first four lines and the second four lines. (I highlight the word *quatrain* and stick to it from now on.)

   ■ How does the change in imagery from hogs and dogs to monsters bring the reader into a new realm, a new kind of story?

   ■ How do the images introduced in the second quatrain affect the characterization of the oppressors and the oppressed? What effect does the diction—words like "nobly" and "kinsmen"—have on the imagery of battle? How does it change the reader's perception of the role of those who were once "hunted and penned"?

   ■ How does the speaker use direct addresses to intensify his call to arms in the third quatrain?

   ■ How do variations in imagery in each of these parts affect the volume or pace of the poem, which reads like a speech at times?

   Again, this is a good time to highlight the term *tone* and demonstrate its meaning with the useful technique of reading poems aloud as a tool for interpretation. For example, have students listen to the vocal difference between the plea of the first quatrain and the command in the final couplet.

   Circulate, encouraging students to use Key Terms and Think-Aloud Prompts as they speak to each other. Model these terms as well.

9. After debriefing their findings, explain that the couplet is the *volta*, a turn, which is found in all forms of the sonnet. The turn or major change in ideas occurs in the final couplet of an English Shakespearean sonnet like McKay's. Ask them to consider how this final couplet works in the scheme of the argument and how it might sound out loud.

10. To end their close reading, it is always good practice to have students compose their thoughts in writing before a final large group debrief. As an alternative to assessing a few of your most skilled apprentices orally, quick-writing is a way of assessing that

every student has understood the lesson. Here are some useful questions for a quick-write:

- What argument is the speaker making to his or her listeners?
- How do the author's choices, such as image, word choice, the sonnet form, and punctuation, affect the rhetorical tone of the persona delivering this text orally?

Lesson Step 7.2: Getting Ready to Recite "If We Must Die"

Teacher-to-Teacher Note. Recitation is a wonderful way to acquaint students with the inner workings of this poem and to build on the initial recitation exercises. I suggest using ad hoc group recitations in class. A workout for the performer, the recitation requires physical intensity and rapid vocal changes in *inflection* (tone or pitch changes in spoken language). Before sharing and reviewing the Getting Ready to Recite: "If We Must Die" assignment (handout 7.A), explore the concept of inflection using the exercise below.

1. Before they begin work with the McKay poem itself, have students use the readers theater exercise below.

   - Visualize the sentences below as if they were spoken into a voice-graphing machine. Have volunteers say the first sentence as an example as you graph it. Ask: Would the line start low and rise or start high and fall? Would it look like a "u" or an "n" or something in between?

   Example: "Are you sure?" might go _____ _____ /
   or this _____ / − .

   Now try these:

   Oh, hello!

   Oh, hello?

   Uh helloooo!

   Alright, if you insist.

   (Adapted from Tanner, *Readers Theatre* 85)

2. Have students break into small groups and go back over the poem as they did in the previous step, sounding out the inflection of each phrase, line, and sentence in order to graph out the lines, indicating their rise and fall. Thicker lines may be used to indicate an increase in the overall emotional intensity of line as well.

3. Have each group divide the poem for an ad hoc recitation and compare their findings. The vocal drama the poet has created is based on increasing levels of rhetorical intensity at each new quatrain. Drawing on the grand tradition of English poetic forms

and dramatic images of the epic, McKay adapts these elements of classical literature to address a modern social crisis. The performers must create stage presence that is up to the task. Have performers rehearse a few times and consider how they will use pace, volume, and gesture to heighten the audience's sensitivity to this masterpiece. Individual performers who wish to prepare formal recitations may be interested in the student handout Getting Ready to Recite: "If We Must Die" (handout 7.A in the appendix).

Lesson Step 7.3: Exploring the English Sonnet through Imitation

Teacher-to-Teacher Note. Like the recitation exercise, this is an opportunity to climb into a sonnet and explore its architecture, the next stop on this 360-degree tour of the text. In this exercise, students will gain a more intimate knowledge of the form and its techniques along with new appreciation for the hard work of other sonneteers. If you have not spent a great deal of time on creative writing in class and are concerned about the difficulty of students' writing in a form, I can promise you that writing in a form is sometimes surprisingly reassuring to students, especially for those who have not written much before. The lack of focus on rhyme and rhythm in this assignment also frees students to focus on just what they have been learning about in all the lessons in the previous chapter—images and the ideas they communicate. As the student handout suggests, for this exercise, students will focus on the development of the parts of an argument.

1. Introduce the idea that being vivid is the main goal of any initial work in creative writing. Pointing to examples of vivid imagery from the class's "Still I Rise" poem or referencing other good work by class poets is useful here!

2. Provide students with the assignment Artful Writing: Exploring the English (Shakespearean) Sonnet (handout 7.B in the appendix), and review it. Then provide class time for initial drafting. For those students who are ready to experiment with rhythm, it is useful to point out that these poems are written in iambic pentameter. (Five feet of iambs!)

3. Have students complete drafts at home. I recommend then having pre-workshop revisions take place in the classroom, as it may be the first time students have attempted writing in sophisticated form; they need the expert advice and reassurance you can offer.

4. The workshop is an essential culminating activity for this exercise. It gives students a chance to improve their piece, work cooperatively as critical friends, and employ their close reading skills for authentic purposes. Best of all, when their peers begin referring to

their work in the same terms they used with published authors, their self-esteem as writers grows by leaps and bounds. Use the Workshop Templates and lesson step 5.4 in this chapter.

5. When students have polished their drafts, provide opportunities for them to publish or share. Once again, if this is a full-blown creative writing unit, make it the goal of every student to publish at least one of their poems in a class book, a school literary journal, a class website, the school newspaper, or other media outlets such as the NCTE's National Gallery of Writing. Have students put together a slam or a performance of some sort and make it special.

More Poems for Practice

Use any of the strategies of this lesson with "Sonnet 130 (My Mistress's Eyes Are Nothing like the Sun)" by William Shakespeare (some difficult language, yet accessible to most high school students), "Joy Sonnet in a Random Universe" by Helen Chasin (easy language, yet the sonnet can be more difficult than Shakespeare in some ways because it is so abstract), and "Sonnet to a Negro in Harlem" by Helen Johnson (challenging yet accessible to most high school students with support). To assess struggling students' understanding of the sonnet form, have students work independently or in small groups to read Shakespeare's love poem, "Sonnet 130," and put it into their own words. Then have them summarize the speaker's sentiments in a few sentences before making a written claim as to whether or not this is a persuasive argument made by a man in love. On-level students might describe the development of the argument of Shakespeare's sonnet, noting the SOAPSTone and the speaker's appeals. Students should support their claims using the details of the text. Advanced students should describe one of the poems, discussing the similarities and differences in the poet's use of diction, imagery, details, form, or tone in each distinct part in the context of the argument he or she makes in the sonnet. They should write in paragraph form.

More Close Reading, Performance, and Powerful Writing Ideas

Close Reading

Have students find a sonnet, complete the following template, and support the claim with evidence from the text: "_____ selects and arranges images of _____ and (other formal elements) to build his or her argument about/for _____." (Sample: Claude McKay selects and arranges images of rural farm life and familiar European legends to build his argument for fighting against oppression, even when the odds of winning are slim.)

Performance

Students may apply performance techniques from this lesson to great speeches from history. Applying the close reading skills students have developed so far to preparing performances of nonfiction is an excellent way of developing critical reading skills across disciplines.

Artful Writing

Students may develop a love sonnet or a satirical sonnet, using the "My Mistress's Eyes Are Nothing like the Sun." I often had students write sonnets to college admissions officers or parents to enhance the focus on argument. See the student sample on the Artful Writing handout from this lesson as a model (see handout 8.A in the appendix).

Lesson 8: Other Sonic Patterns

Teacher-to-Teacher Note. In "Those Winter Sundays," Robert Hayden uses concrete imagery, allusion, alliteration, assonance, and consonance in a masterful unrhymed sonnet written in iambic pentameter. Because this tour de force offers such fine examples of so many of the devices and techniques students have studied, I spend a great deal of time helping students see each layer of this magnificently united work of language art. Though the amount of reading and rereading I ask students to do here might seem daunting, the poem's subject—the challenges of the parent-child relationship—resonates with many students, and the seemingly simple poem offers itself so teachably to students. For reliable sources of the text, see "Additional Resources for Chapter 3" at the end of the chapter.

Lesson Step 8.1: Exploring Connections between Images and Sonic Patterns

1. *Frontloading Knowledge Option*: Have students research various tellings and images of the story of Kronos, the legend of Greek myth, and Jesus, the central figure of Christian theology. Have students create a Venn diagram, detailing the similarities and differences in the father and son relationships between these two tales. Tell students that by choosing certain words or images, poets are granting us license to bring associations to our readings, including subtle allusions to famous stories, which act as master narratives in our culture. Since these master narratives are so pervasive in our culture, writers can count on our knowledge of them and invite us to make those associations in very subtle ways.

2. Have students take a moment to perform a quick-write about a vivid memory of an adult who played an important role in their childhood (parent, older sibling, aunt, etc.). Have students try to flesh out in as much detail as possible the one image they think of when they think of that person. The image should be recorded in sensory descriptions. (Sample: I remember my mother wrapping me in her winter coat, covering me in her warmth, as we walked to school on a blustery day.) Have students pair and share their memories. In a large group debrief, have students discuss the nature of memories, noting which details are remembered and which are forgotten when it comes to the people closest to us. Let students know that they will be studying a poem that deals with memory and reflection, analyzing the key images that the author has chosen for the speaker's reflection.

3. As always, have students take out their Key Literary Terms for Discussing Poetic Forms and Techniques and Think-Aloud Prompts handouts. Share the poem and have students perform a close reading. As they practice their routine of visualization, students should sketch each image on paper. This visualization activity will highlight the images of the father, bent over and working in the dark, and the son, rising and dressing in the light and warmth. Be sure to ask students to draw the setting, indicating details such as the weather, the time of day, household activity, and so on. Remind them that it is important to look for patterns and variations. In this poem, it is interesting to highlight the pattern of contrasts between fire and winter ice, as well as night and day, Sundays and weekdays, fathers and sons, past and present, and so on. As always, have them identify the antecedent scenario, the SOAPSTone, and the divisions or major parts. As you circulate, remind students once again to practice using key terms in their discussions and making interpretive claims, while supporting them with specific references to the text.

4. Project the text for dividing and annotating the poem as a class. Then in a large group debrief have students share their findings, including their illustrations and their ideas about the rhetorical situations in the poem.

    Ask students whether they have identified any allusions. With effective frontloading, some students can see the subtle connection between the stories of Kronos and Jesus in Hayden's father–son story. The idea that the father is polishing his son's shoes on a Sunday suggests the idea of the Sunday best—church-going clothes. A much more subtle allusion can be found in the word "offices," which refers to a particular station within Christian religious hierarchies. Both words link readers to the Christian narrative of Jesus, the sacrificial Son of God. The word "chronic," which originates from the Greek root for the word *time*, alludes to the story of Kronos, a patricidal son whose plans to kill his own potentially patricidal children backfire.

Next, remind students that sonnets are not all rhymed. Some students will have already noted that the poem is fourteen lines long and written in iambic pentameter (therefore, a sonnet). Have students consider the reasons for these stanza breaks in the context of their knowledge of stanzas by asking how each part responds to the part that came before it. How are the last two lines of this sonnet related to the rest? How are they similar to and different from a volta in an English sonnet?

5. Now for the focus of the lesson: sonic patterns. Just as the lumbering verb choices of "got up" and "put on" contrast with the ease of the verbs "rise" and "dress," there is a contrast in the actual sounds associated with the father and the son. Model, using the first stanza, how one might look for sonic patterns by highlighting repeated sounds. After highlighting repetitions such as the hard *k* pattern that begins in the second line, have students assist in highlighting the repeated sounds (hard *k*, *b*, *z*, etc.). There are many good examples of alliteration, assonance, and consonance in the poem. Have students carry on in small groups with the remainder of the poem; then return to a large group discussion with an analysis of the ways in which the sonic drama connects to the emotional drama.

As a final flourish, tell students that all of Shakespeare's sonnets contain a key word, a word that acts as the nexus for all sorts of elements in the poem. Ask them to examine the poem and select a word they would nominate as the key word. I would nominate "chronic," but students may have other valid reasons for nominating another word. It is just a great discussion to end the lesson. (Here is a case for *chronic*. Not only does *chronic* link us to the story of Kronos, but it provides part of the underlying pattern of time/cycle references and, best of all, acts as a sonic nexus of sorts, connecting a pattern of sound so carefully woven throughout the text.) (See Helen Vendler's *The Art of Shakespeare's Sonnets* for more on the concept of key words. She discusses a key word in each explication.)

Lesson Step 8.2: Getting Ready to Recite "Those Winter Sundays" through Group Performance Activities

Teacher-to-Teacher Note. Students may refer to any of the techniques in earlier recitation exercises, especially the *Build, Crisis, Climax, Dénouement* analyses, as they prepare recitations. However, a group performance exercise that capitalizes on their attention to the sounds of words offers the class a chance to collaborate once again, a great way to lay the groundwork for the grand class performance I suggest as a culminating activity for the performance and imitative writing leg of this 360-degree tour of poetry.

For recitation lesson steps and handouts, see my lesson "Speaking Poetry: Exploring Sonic Patterns through Performance" at the

ReadWriteThink website (http://www.readwritethink.org/classroom-resources/lesson-plans/speaking-poetry-exploring-sonic-1158.html).

Lesson Step 8.3: Exploring Sonic Patterns through Imitation—A Culminating Lesson and Reflection

Teacher-to-Teacher Note. By the end of this leg of the 360-degree tour, students have developed a keener sense of what it takes to be a good reader, a good writer, and a good critical friend for peers who write. I set my expectations fairly high on this particular piece of creative writing, and students, in my experience, rise to the challenge. As always, I ask students to focus first on being vivid (regardless of which of two options they choose), but I also ask them to take a shot at attending to more technical choices as they revise. In order to gain the full benefit of transference into academic writing, I want them to process multiple ways of expressing themselves, discovering various routes to putting the best words in the best order. The highlight of this lesson for me is always the revision process.

Finally, whether or not you are only planning to use creative writing as a "unit," it is important to build in reflection time for students to consider what they have gained through the experience of exploring literature through the eyes of the writer. The last step in this lesson suggests ways to wrap up this workshop with such a reflection.

1. Present the student handout Artful Writing: Creating Sonic Patterns (handout 8.A in the appendix) and review it. As always, have students begin drafting in class and complete the writing at home.

2. Have students revise in class in small group and whole group workshops using the Workshop Templates (handout 5.E in the appendix). See also "Facilitating Peer Workshops," lesson step 5.4 in this chapter, for tips on facilitating the workshop. As I mentioned in the discussion of workshops in Chapter 1, it is essential that every student experience the whole group workshop at least once. Be conscious of those who have dodged this so far. Also, be sure to hear from those who have not shared their feedback with the whole group in previous whole group workshops. Practice making evaluative or interpretive claims about writing is essential in scaffolding the skill of claim making for academic arguments.

3. Remember to have students publish or perform this or another piece in a big-deal performance.

4. Have students reflect upon their 360-degree tour. While these questions can be used to reflect on each exercise, they can also be used at the end of the unit. A simple letter is a great way to

give you and your students a chance to think about the opportunities and challenges of this process. Honoring the highlights and lowlights of this experience is also an important part of the process of helping our students become independent learners. Here are samples of reflection questions I have used in the past:

- Describe one high and one low in your experience with using poems as a springboard to your own creative writing.

- Describe a moment in reading or rereading a poem when you appreciated the aptness of a writer's choice of word, image, technique, or form.

- Describe a moment when you went back to a poem in the composition or revision of your own piece, to see more carefully what the other poet did. Perhaps it was a moment when a particular poem came to mind, inspiring an idea, an image, a word choice, or a technique. Perhaps it was a moment when you, the writer, felt the need to reread a poem in order to understand better the author's craft.

- Describe a moment when revision was difficult and one in which it was particularly satisfying.

- Describe a moment when a workshop was useful in your revision process and one in which you felt useful in someone else's revision process.

- Describe a moment when you felt that you, as a reader, writer, or peer, really owned a key literary term and could use it with confidence.

More Poems for Practice

"We Real Cool" by Gwendolyn Brooks (brief and rich), "Let Evening Come" by Jane Kenyon (accessible but more difficult), and "Digging" by Seamus Heaney (more challenging but the perfect companion piece for this skill lesson) are excellent examples of poems that capitalize on sonic patterns. The language of each of these poems is fairly accessible to most high school readers, but they are all technically rich, so I have to admit I hesitated to label them according to level of difficulty here. To assess students at lower levels of readiness, ask them to use different colored highlighters to highlight sonic patterns in one of the poems above and write a description of the pattern that they see. Also ask them to hypothesize in writing at least one connection between a sonic element and another element of the poem, such as image, idea, or tone, and share it with peers in a small group discussion to be observed by you. Have on-level students extend this activity by writing a brief explanation of how a particular sound or sonic element relates to sense, based on connections to images and ideas in the poem. Advanced students might write an extended response, detailing the relationship between sound and sense throughout a poem.

More Close Reading, Performance, and Powerful Writing Ideas

Close Reading

Have students complete the following template and use it as a claim for a paragraph about a poem in which the poet has exploited sonic patterns for meaningful effect: The poet _____ creates a pattern of _____ to highlight the connection between _____ and _____ in his or her poem. (Sample: The poet Robert Hayden creates a pattern of consonant sounds to highlight the connection between images of the father's hard work and his hard love.)

Performance

Have students watch a reading or performance of any of the suggested poems and discuss how the reader/performer heightens the audience's awareness of the sonic patterning. Readings and recitations of all these poems are available online, and each is an example of how one might perform a poem. Then have students apply their heightened attention to sonic patterns to their own performances of published or original poems.

Artful Writing

Have students revise an earlier piece of their writing with attention to sonic patterns. Have them select something that is old enough to allow them to look at it with fresh eyes. Whether it is poetry or prose, have students consider how sound might enhance the piece.

Additional Resources for Chapter 3

Poems, Poets, Poetry

"'Hope' is the thing with feathers" by Emily Dickinson
  - Audio of the poem
    http://www.reelyredd.com/dickinson08.hope.htm
  - Using the poem as an example of how to read line breaks
    http://poetryoutloud.org/audio/21%20Form%20And%20Free%20Verse%20Emily%20Dickinson.mp3

"I Am Waiting" by Lawrence Ferlinghetti
  - *Poetry Foundation,*
    http://www.poetryfoundation.org/poem/171598

"Those Winter Sundays" by Robert Hayden

- ■ Discussion of the poem in "Poetry off the Shelf," includes a reading of the poem by Hayden; other poems discussed as well
  http://www.poetryfoundation.org/journal/audioitem.html?id=1648
- ■ Animated poem read by Carl Hancock Rux
  http://www.poetryfoundation.org/journal/videoitem.html?id=36

"If We Must Die" by Claude McKay

- ■ A reading of the poem
  http://www.archive.org/details/ClaudeMckayIfWeMustDie_3

Other Reliable Sources of Texts

- ■ www.poetryfoundation.org
- ■ www.poets.org
- ■ www.bartleby.com

Reading Poems and Poetry

Birkerts, Sven. *Readings*. St. Paul: Graywolf, 1999. Print.

Bloom, Harold. *The Art of Reading Poetry*. New York: Perennial, 2005. Print.

Burt, Stephen. *Close Calls with Nonsense: Reading New Poetry*. Saint Paul: Graywolf, 2009. Print.

Hirsch, Edward. *How to Read a Poem: And Fall in Love with Poetry*. Orlando: Harvest, 1999. Print.

Hollander, John. *Rhyme's Reason: A Guide to English Verse*. New Haven: Yale UP, 2001. Print.

Pinsky, Robert. *The Sounds of Poetry: A Brief Guide*. New York: Farrar, 2000. Print.

Powell, Joseph, and Mark Halperin. *Accent on Meter: A Handbook for Readers of Poetry*. Urbana: NCTE, 2004. Print.

Simmons, Russell, prod. "Def Poetry." *Russell Simmons Presents Def Poetry: Seasons 1–6*. Home Box Office. Television.

Slam Nation. Dir. Paul Devlin. Perf. Mychelle Dee and Craig MuMs Grant. New Video Group, 2005. DVD.

Strand, Mark, and Eavan Boland. *The Making of a Poem: A Norton Anthology of Poetic Forms*. New York: Norton, 2001. Print.

Tanner, Fran Averett. *Readers Theatre Fundamentals: A Cumulative Approach to Theory and Activities*. Topeka: Clark, 1993. Print.

Vendler, Helen. *The Music of What Happens: Poems, Poets, Critics*. Cambridge: Harvard UP, 1995. Print.

Writing Poems and Facilitating Writing Workshops

Dunning, Stephen, and William Stafford. *Getting the Knack: 20 Poetry Writing Exercises*. Urbana: NCTE, 1992. Print.

Fagin, Larry. *The List Poem: A Guide to Teaching and Writing Catalog Verse*. New York: Teachers and Writers Collaborative, 2000. Print.

Hermsen, Terry. *Poetry of Place: Helping Students Write Their Worlds*. Urbana: NCTE, 2009. Print.

Michaels, Judith Rowe. *Risking Intensity: Reading and Writing Poetry with High School Students*. Urbana: NCTE, 1999. Print.

O'Connor, John S. *Wordplaygrounds: Reading, Writing, and Performing Poetry in the English Classroom*. Urbana: NCTE, 2004. Print.

Oliver, Mary. *Rules for the Dance: A Handbook for Writing and Reading Metrical Verse*. Boston: Houghton, 1998. Print.

Padgett, Ron. *The Teachers and Writers Handbook of Poetic Forms*. New York: Teachers and Writers Collaborative, 2000. Print.

Statman, Mark. *Listener in the Snow: The Practice and Teaching of Poetry*. New York: Teachers and Writers Collaborative, 2003. Print.

Theune, Michael. *Structure and Surprise: Engaging Poetic Turns*. New York: Teachers and Writers Collaborative, 2007. Print.

Tufte, Virginia. *Artful Sentences: Syntax as Style*. Cheshire: Graphics P, 2006. Print.

Vendler, Helen H., ed. *The Art of Shakespeare's Sonnets*. Cambridge: Harvard UP, 1999. Print.

4 Representing Close Readings in Academic Writing

Poems as a Springboard for Academic Argument

While I use performance and creative writing in part to enrich students' lives with the sheer pleasures of literature and artful self-expression, I also use these strategies simply because they are effective. Not only are they the underused bridge between students' interests and their best interests, they are, I would argue, in some cases the most useful strategies for learning about literature, as they challenge readers to make meaning of texts in ways that traditional read/discuss/write approaches miss. There is, after all, a fundamental difference between the cognitive experience of describing a speaker's utterance and attempting to physicalize it, between learning about an aspect of an author's craft and trying one's hand at it. These approaches to text need not be exclusive, nor should they always be preferred over others; but in terms of academic outcomes—if critical reading and writing skills are ultimately what we seek to develop—they should not be viewed as frivolous either.

This chapter, which exploits these approaches in service of the academic essay, makes explicit my rationale for using all aspects of the 360-degree approach to teaching literature—engaging students through performance (sometimes the closest of readings), creative writing (a most deliberate kind of writing), and academic argument (expressing the findings of a close reading in powerful ways). This range of approaches offers many opportunities for students to access and work with text at various levels.

The key questions in this sequence focus on the sentence level—the verb and other sentence parts. As with aspects of image and form explored in earlier chapters, describing the sentence-level choices that make up the art of a poem requires additional vocabulary. With each new term—agency, syntax, sentence type, speech act, and so forth—students will acquire a new gateway to comprehension and pleasure, and a greater command of the language of academic discourse. This sentence-level knowledge is essential for understanding and composing their own explications and other academic arguments about texts.

Here is how this chapter works: Using everything they have learned so far about how to construct and represent the meaning of a poem through performance and informal descriptions (Think-Aloud Prompts and Workshop Templates), students will perform close readings and (optional) recitations of four new poems. Moving from the informal claims they practiced in think-alouds and workshops, students will explore more formal academic claims in sample explications. By using the Describing Text Templates (handout 9.D in the appendix) as a lens to explore sample explications that are provided, students will also have ample opportunity to engage with the kind of writing they will be asked to produce, so they can see fluent uses of the language they will employ in describing text. Ultimately, they will write and revise their own explication, using the Describing Text Templates, to scaffold their own fluent use of academic language.

The analysis and claim-making skills students gain in their practice with poetry will prepare them to make arguments about other kinds of texts, from essays to religious and political documents, as well as works of art. Yet regardless of the topic, the foundation of the strongest claims is a deep understanding of multiple perspectives. To move students forward to practice such rich claim making, I end the 360-degree tour with ideas for making the transition from poetry to other genres through debate. Teachers can capitalize on student interest in issues of gender, animal rights, war, and race and ethnicity that are raised by the pre-reading activities, discussions, and dueling recitations in this chapter. Further research into any of these questions opens opportunities to extend claim-making fluency with texts from other genres that represent multiple perspectives on these compelling issues. With plenty of fruit-bearing practice in talking the talk, and writing the talk, students will be poised to develop arguments across genres, while continuing to find new challenges that come with learning the nuances and language of each discipline or genre.

A final note about differentiation in this chapter: While the lesson steps provide the focus of the instruction and the "More Poems for Practice" section provides suggested texts for different levels of readiness, the assessment tasks are not varied. At this point, all students should be challenged to write about texts at their own accessibility level, and they should be provided with appropriate levels of peer and instructor support and adequate time to improve the fluency and complexity of their claims and supports. Instructors may also vary the evaluation criteria to accommodate varying levels of readiness; however, throughout this chapter I recommend that everyone follow the same process and produce the same product, as formal academic writing is essential to college and career readiness.

Lesson 9: Analyzing How Agency Shapes Meaning in a Poem

Teacher-to-Teacher Note. "They Flee from Me" by Sir Thomas Wyatt is one of my favorite poems to teach and a favorite among students as well—well, that is, after they get past their initial fears of the archaic language. The focus of this lesson is to understand how verbs function in a sentence or phrase and to analyze how writers manipulate them. Being able to notice *agency*—recognizing who is performing the action—is one of the surest ways for students to become more powerful readers and writers. If the archaic language of "They Flee from Me" presents too great a barrier to entry for students, use one of the widely accessible poems in the "More Poems for Practice" menu at the end of this lesson. But don't shy away from verb analysis, regardless of the levels at which your students are working.

Depending upon how much direct instruction they have received in grammar, students will have varying levels of confidence in discussing different aspects of verbs. However, most students I've encountered, even the very young or struggling, can identify action words in a text, which is the easiest place to begin. And if they can get that far, they can usually answer the question, "Who is doing the action?" To discover the art of a poem via agency, one begins by answering those two questions: "What is the action?" and "Who is performing it?"

After applying what they already know about getting the gist of a poem (visualizing imagery, looking for the antecedent scenario, dividing the poem into parts, and identifying key aspects of the rhetorical situation or SOAPSTone), students will deepen their understanding of the text by practicing the new strategy of analyzing agency. Armed with a sophisticated understanding of the poem and an advanced vocabulary, they will then read a sample explication before making their own sophisticated claims about the art of a poem. For reliable sources for the poem's text see "Additional Resources for Chapter 4" at the end of this chapter.

Lesson Step 9.1: Understanding Agency

1. *Frontloading Knowledge Option:* Have students complete a prereading quick-write in response to the following questions: "Some say that a leopard can't change its spots. Is this true? Is the nature of a person determined at birth, a destiny of sorts that cannot be

escaped? Or can people change?" Facilitate a group discussion of student findings before reading the poem. Let students know that they will have a chance to explore these questions further as they listen in on a speaker's reflections about past relationships.

I also share a little background about the poet. (They love to hear about this guy!) Sir Thomas Wyatt lived in the first half of the sixteenth century and traveled throughout Europe as an ambassador for Henry VIII, who eventually had Wyatt imprisoned on suspicion that he was having an affair with Anne Boleyn, the queen who was famously beheaded by her husband. (By the way, an HBO series called *The Tudors* includes a snippet of this intriguing story.)

In Wyatt's "They Flee from Me," one of the most anthologized poems of the British Renaissance, the jilted lover recounts his wins and losses in the battle of the sexes, revealing the many dimensions of his character through his artful manipulation of agency. (For more background, search the Web for Sir Thomas Wyatt's incredibly interesting biography and for word histories, especially for the words *range*, *hart*, *newfangledness*, and *hath*.) For students who would have difficulty tackling this text, model a fluent reading or have a talented performer recite the poem before beginning a close reading and analysis. A one-sentence summary of the poem also helps set the stage for understanding. For example, "In this poem, the speaker is reflecting on his past relationships with women and tells us about one special woman in particular."

2. Let students know that the goal of this next sequence is to explore the art of a poem at the sentence level. In this case, exploring the verbs will help them get a better handle on this character. Distribute and review Key Literary Terms for Discussing the Verb and Other Sentence Parts (handout 9.A in the appendix). Tell students they will be taking a close look at agency in this poem and project these two sentences:

- The *agent* of action is the performer of the action.
- "The sun rose."

Introduce the idea that just as they used other keys to exploring a poem—knowledge of various aspects of imagery and form—they will now begin exploring verbs and other sentence parts to deepen their understanding of poets' choices at the sentence and phrase level. Tell them that they will begin by examining verbs (actions or states of being), and then they will look for the agents (the performers of the actions) and consider how other parts of a sentence fall around those two essential components. Using the example sentence "The sun rose," ask students:

- What is the action of this sentence? (rose)
- Who performed the action of rising? (sun)

Explain that since poets can construct a sentence in countless ways, it is sometimes useful to take a careful look at the agency in each image, noting who has been given control over an action. It is especially useful in this poem, as the drama lies in the most ancient battle for control, the battle of the sexes.

3. Project fluent and sophisticated student utterances as examples of students producing evidence-based claims. You can refer to these student utterances later as samples of the kind of claim making the Describing Text Templates support, demonstrating that explication is merely a more formal piece of writing based on the same kind of work they have been doing all along.

   Distribute the poem and demonstrate how to do a different kind of close reading, one that focuses on the agent of action. Provide a model think-aloud with the first two lines. This is especially important because the archaic syntax of Wyatt's sentences can be difficult. I project the first sentence, "They flee from me that sometime did me seek / With naked foot, stalking in my chamber," and do a think-aloud:

   > I am going to look for the verbs (or action words) first and underline them.

   Have students take over or at least assist.

   > As I begin visualizing these images, the words "Flee" and "seek" <u>make me picture</u> a chase. "Stalking" is <u>another interesting word</u> choice. <u>That diction makes me think</u> of a predator and prey. <u>It makes me think</u> of animals.
   >
   > Now I am going to look for agency or who is doing each of the actions. "They" is doing the fleeing. I am going to circle the agent "They."

   Have students assist again, by asking who is doing the seeking. After they identify the speaker as the agent, it gets a little tricky.

   > The order of sentence parts, or the sentence's syntax, makes it hard to tell whose foot is naked and who did the stalking, so I'll have to read on to find out more about the actors and actions and come back to make a better guess about that.

   Have students continue on their own in small groups, underlining every verb and circling the agent or the owner of each action—not just the main verb of the sentence, but each image, every line, and every clause. As they work, have each group jot down a line-by-line paraphrase.

4. As you circulate, model Key Literary Terms for Discussing the Verb and Other Sentence Parts, as well as other *key terms*. Be sure each individual student has success in identifying verbs and their agents. Believe me, being able to talk with students about verbs and their agents, using a common vocabulary, will make future writers conferences, student writing workshops, and critical discussions of text exponentially more productive.

5. Bring the whole group together to get the gist of the poem. As always, have students identify the SOAPSTone and the antecedent scenario and complete a few paraphrasings. (Critical essays about the poem make for more interesting discussions. *Laura*, a book by Barbara L. Estrin, is a wonderful source for more on this. Though the text is written for a scholarly audience, certain passages might be shared productively with students to deepen their discussion. Sharing manageable portions of challenging texts will make scholarship seem less foreign, and this is a great time to do it.)

6. Suggest to students that taking a closer look at their findings about agency may help them to learn more about the character who is telling the story. Project the text and record group findings regarding agent and action. Next, model an analysis of agency in a think-aloud of the remaining lines of the first stanza, as always, asking students to assist.

> Let's think about what our findings about agency reveal about this character . . .
>
> "I have seen them gentle, tame, and meek." So the speaker, "I," is performing the action. He has "seen" them. His <u>diction</u> here is really interesting: "gentle, tame, and meek." The word "tame" <u>is making me think</u> of animals again.

Have students assist with the next line.

> Can someone share a think-aloud of the rest of this stanza?

Students often point to other animal imagery: "wild," "put themself in danger / To take bread at my hand," "range," "busily seeking." (You may need to define *range*, which means to wander freely.)

> <u>These descriptions make me think</u> that the speaker has a pretty superior attitude toward women. Let's look at the verbs in the second stanza to see if this hypothesis is true.

The opening of the second stanza is almost verb-free. "Thanked be" and "Hath been" are the only verbs in the first four lines, until "did fall," and the agent of this action verb just happens to be none other than a woman's gown. To help students explore possible reasons why the speaker delays this verb, ask them these questions:

> What effect does the delay have in terms of the imagery unfolding? How does the verb count of the second half of the stanza compare with the first half? Who is performing the actions? What does that suggest about who is in charge in this stanza?

Students usually point out that the author's use of verbs has changed in some way, even if they don't get this sophisticated in their readings:

The delayed verb in the gown image creates a sense of anticipation, and the rapid succession of verbs in the second half
of the stanza creates the sense of motion, as if the speaker is
remembering a whirlwind romance. Students will observe that
the female character is explicitly developed in a different way
than the women in the first stanza, who were described in verbs
that suggest animalistic qualities rather than human ones.

7. As students explore this second stanza, highlight once again
how useful it is to use one's voice as an interpretive instrument
by having them play with the question "Dear heart, how like
you this?" Have them explore how various intonations of the
last two words lead to very different questions. (*Do you like what
I am doing?* Or *Ha! How do you like being treated this way?*)

8. Continue exploring Wyatt's use of agency in the last stanza. Have
students wrap up their analysis using an in-class writing before
debriefing their findings using these questions:

> Based on your close look at agency, who seems to be in control
> of the action at various points in the poem? Compare the agents
> of action in the first, second, and third stanzas. What is the
> effect of shifting control of agency from one party to another
> in each part of the poem? What do these changes reveal about
> the situation or the speaker's attitude toward women? What
> is the speaker's attitude toward women in this last stanza?
> Toward this woman in particular? How might he view himself
> in relation to women as a result of this relationship?

Optional Lesson Step—Dueling Recitations of "They Flee from Me"

Teacher-to-Teacher Note. After the wonderful debate this poem inevitably
causes in class discussions, dueling recitations are great fun, especially
if you have some generous performers. Have several students prepare
ad hoc or full-blown recitations or rehearse staged readings to explore
the shifts in tone that accompany the character's shifting attitude toward
women. It heightens everyone's appreciation of the poem and illustrates
the importance of reading poems aloud to get closer to meaning.

1. Use the student handout Getting Ready to Recite: "They Flee
from Me" (handout 9.B in the appendix) as a guide, and remind
performers to apply strategies from previous recitation lessons
as they work up their performances.

2. Have students debrief performances, discussing whether the
speaker has or has not actually had a change of heart about
women. Also consider whether or not he accepts responsibility
for his role in botching relationships.

Lesson Step 9.2: Ad Hoc Debates

This mini-lesson gives students a chance to practice orally the kind of writing they will do in explication, making claims and supporting them with text. After the dueling performances or debate-oriented closing discussions, have students gather in groups of four. Larger groups or even half the class can do this exercise as well, if that makes more sense for you and your students. While smaller groups allow for more opportunities for individual speakers *to experience the genuine need to employ critical reading skills to win*, students who have never debated before might need a few trial runs with the support of the whole group. Also, if the ad hoc debate format doesn't work for you, more formal formats and rubrics are available online.

1. Assign one team an affirmative position and have the other team take the negative position on the following resolution: The speaker in Sir Thomas Wyatt's "They Flee from Me" was profoundly changed by his encounter with this special woman.

2. Give teams a few minutes to construct a claim. Have them provide at least two reasons to support the claim and defend those reasons with one or two specific references to the text.

3. Have one member of each team present their claims and supporting evidence in a two-minute opening argument. The opposing teams should listen carefully, jotting down notes for revising rebuttals.

    Let students know that their responsiveness to their opponent's arguments will make up a major part of their team's grade or score. This can be formal or informal, depending on how much time you want to spend on it. In the most basic, ad hoc situations, I have simply given a score of zero to two (Not really, 0; Sort of, 1; Definitely, 2) on each of four criteria:

    - Student clearly stated valid claims.
    - Student used valid textual evidence effectively.
    - Student predicted or responded effectively to counterarguments.
    - Student employed language effectively to communicate arguments powerfully.

4. After listening to initial arguments, give teams a chance to huddle before another member of each team presents rebuttals.

5. The final segment of the debate is the closing arguments, in which a member of each team has a chance to wrap up the team's argument and sharpen the delivery of main points and counterpoints.

6. Many adolescents enjoy the friendly competition of debate. Reflect on the debate process as a whole group. Point out how

the skills they have been learning in their study of poetry might apply to all sorts of academic arguments. In academia, after all, well-constructed claims and well-developed reasoning, grounded in text or data, wins in all aspects of academic, professional, and public discourse.

Lesson Step 9.3: Writing an Explication—Summary Drafting

Teacher-to-Teacher Note. After so much informal practice in describing text, it is time for students to write more formal descriptions of poems, otherwise known as explications. With the benefit of modeling, hands-on practice, and the vocabulary they have acquired, students are more than capable of reading and making sophisticated claims about text. This lesson step introduces the idea of summary as the opening part of an explication, which is a detailed walk-through that describes the art of a poem.

1. Distribute the handout Developing Summaries of Poems (handout 9.C in the appendix), along with the following question to guide students as they draft formal summaries of the Wyatt poem: "What is the story this poem tells (in a nutshell)?" Have students pair up, share their summaries, and then revise them. After revising, have a few pairs share their summaries with the entire class. Using the criteria in the handout, conduct an abbreviated whole class revision workshop to create models of whole poem summaries for the Wyatt poem. See the Chapter 1 section titled "How Can We Facilitate Writers Workshops with Artistic and Academic Benefits" for additional information on facilitating a whole class workshop. Have students record these models for reference in their notebooks.

2. Ask students to select a poem they feel comfortable discussing in writing. The poems in the "More Poems for Practice" section of each lesson might be a good list from which to draw, but the poetry websites highlighted in "Additional Resources for Chapter 4" offer plenty of quality poems for students to choose, and the process of surfing and picking a poem is fun and enriching in many other ways.

   Brief narratives and lyrics work best for beginners, but the most important thing for students to keep in mind as they select a poem is that they have to be drawn to the poem genuinely. If they find that they cannot summarize it, even after applying all of the close reading strategies they know, they should consider a more accessible poem. The poems students select will be used in the next several steps, including explication, so students should make sure they have picked a poem that is right for them: accessible, interesting, and so on. Allow students time to apply the close reading strategies they learned in Chapter 2 to gain a basic understanding of their selected poem (visualization, exploring antecedent scenario, dividing the poem into parts, identifying SOAPSTone, and paraphrasing).

3. In class or for homework, have students select a poem and practice summarizing it. If possible, the whole class could have copies of all the poems students may be explicating so that class discussions about student writing make sense. If that is impossible, students ought to read their poems aloud before discussing samples of their writing or workshopping with peers.

4. Have students pair up and revise their summaries. Circulate as they work in pairs, looking for common areas for improvement and selecting samples for a brief whole class workshop.

5. Repeating the abbreviated whole class workshop format, have students share summaries with the class. Use a few samples as the basis of a whole class revision exercise focused on detailed yet precise summarizing sentences that convey some sense of the antecedent scenario and SOAPSTone.

Lesson Step 9.4: Introducing Explication and the Describing Text Templates

Teacher-to-Teacher Note. Assure students that they are prepared to read and write explications of poems. Some students may have previous experience with academic discourse, while others may be reading this kind of text for the first time. Regardless of their level of experience with formal interpretation, remind them that with the extensive vocabulary they have developed thus far in their study of poetry and their deep knowledge of the Wyatt poem, they are more than ready to tackle the project.

While there isn't an exact formula or template for organizing an explication, explications generally do the following:

- Describe the poem from beginning to end rather than feature by feature.
- Focus on one or two techniques or themes and discuss how they are developed throughout the poem.
- Consist of paragraphs corresponding with parts of the poem, which are divided and presented in chronological order.
- Cover a variety of aspects of author's craft and one or more techniques a poet has employed throughout the poem.

It is important to note that with the exception of certain specialized publications, explications of particular poems are frequently not stand-alone academic essays but are often woven into larger arguments about a writer, a writer's entire body of work, or themes and techniques in a particular period, genre, or another kind of collection. Still, we ask students in upper-level high school classes and undergraduate college courses to write this kind of literary analysis, so we should show them how to do it well, lest we add our students' voices to the cries of desperation that can readily be found all over the Internet. Let's face it: fortunes are being made by selling this kind of paper.

1. Project the definition of an explication and share it with students. Here is the definition I use: *An explication is a commentary that walks readers through the meaning of a text by making claims about a poet's choices and supporting them with evidence from the text.* Remind students that they have made oral and written claims and supported them with textual evidence throughout their study of poetry and that they will now learn to formalize their claims in writing.

2. Ask students to take out their Think-Aloud Prompts and Workshop Templates. Have students review the handouts, reminding them that these templates helped them explain to peers how they interpreted the authors' choices in many texts. Then distribute the Describing Text Templates (handout 9.D in the appendix) and point out that making claims in formal academic writing is similar, but rather than speaking directly to the author this time, the audience of an explication is other readers and scholars who are interested in how you have interpreted the poem.

3. Review the templates and discuss similarities and differences between a larger claim and subclaim. Students may note that the associated meanings are not stated in the large claim, but they are clearly implied. In subclaims, meanings are often more explicitly spelled out. If you have recorded samples of sophisticated claims that students have made throughout the discussion, now is a good time to point out the similarities in the underlying format of this kind of claim.

Lesson Step 9.5: Exploring an Explication through the Lens of the Describing Texts Templates

1. Distribute the sample explication of "They Flee from Me" (handout 9.E in the appendix) and let students know that they will be seeing summaries and Describing Text Templates in action as they read this sample.

2. Before assigning the explication to students, be sure they engage in a brief evaluative reading/discussion of the sample, answering SOAPSTone questions. Then share the sample Explication Rubric for reference (handout 9.F).

3. Have students perform an initial reading of the explication. Have them locate the summary and discuss it. Then have them read

actively, marking directly on the page: a heart for *agree* or *good point*; a question mark for *question* or *discuss*; a check for *disagree*. They should then highlight other striking words, phrases, and sentences. Use these markings as a springboard for a discussion about the explication. In the course of your discussion, have a few students share a summary of the argument of the explication. Ask: "What does this explication argue the poem is about? What claims are made about Wyatt's technique?" You might even create a class outline of the explication, highlighting the organization, the reason for paragraph breaks, and so forth in your discussion.

4. Next, using the Describing Text Templates, have students take another close look at the opening paragraph in small groups. Have them identify the large claim and record it on a separate sheet of paper.

5. Next have students label the parts of the large claim according to the template labels—that is, choice maker, choice, and interpreted meaning.

6. Individually, have students label the parts of the subclaims in the first paragraph or two. Again have them record subclaims on a separate sheet of paper and label the parts using the subclaim template language. Remind them that each part of the template may not appear in every sentence, but each part of the claim template is explicitly or implicitly stated somewhere in the text.

7. Have students share these findings in small groups. As you circulate, you should also ask them to think about the organization of the explication; point out how the explication progresses from the beginning to the end of the poem. Once again, check in with each group to ensure every student's engagement.

8. Once you feel confident students are familiar with the process of identifying a claim and its parts, give students a moment to focus on another paragraph and to select and label a subclaim, individually. Collect these individual assignments to assess how well students are able to recognize claims. Individual conferences may be required to help all students learn to identify key elements of explicative writing, as students will soon be constructing their own claims and writing a complete explication. Have students connect evidence from the sample to parts of the rubric in their final discussion about the sample. The rubric is intended to help students understand the constituent parts of this specialized kind of writing. It can be modified over the course of drafts to focus on different aspects each time. A first draft workshop might focus only on "Development and Thematic Discussion." "Evidence" and "Presentation of Evidence" can be the focus of a second workshop. A final workshop can focus on sentence level fluidity and conventions.

Lesson Step 9.6: Constructing a Claim about a Poem

Teacher-to-Teacher Note. I first used the Describing Text Templates to help students develop claims while teaching a senior English literature course. I adapted it with novels, plays, speeches, art, and so on. Through my work in the school's literacy center, I was also invited by other English teachers to share this template in classes throughout our 9–12 curriculum in English. I didn't present it as a formula to be followed exactly, but as prompter to remind students to state explicitly "how they got what they got" out of a text. Though this assignment only asks for a claim, I find that students draft better claims after attempting to write the whole explication. Since it is a brief essay, drafting is an effective approach to deepening student thinking as they construct claims. The Describing Text Think-Sheet activity (handout 9.G in the appendix) in this step is essential, as it helps students think through their claim before they attempt to word it elegantly and concisely. Additional sample sentences from professional writing follow on an optional student handout.

1. Distribute the Describing Text Think-Sheet (handout 9.G) and have students develop original claims about the poems they used in the summarizing exercise in the previous step. Simply ask students to begin by jotting down what they think the poem is about—not the summary, but the commentary or observation the writer seems to be making about the subject, situation, or about the nature of being human. Let students think-write informally, before trying to work with the template. After a brief period of free writing, have them use the Describing Text Think-Sheet to formalize their claims.

2. Many claims about agency may be proposed, given the lesson, but the students shouldn't feel compelled to focus on that aspect. Some students may feel more empowered to make claims about elements of imagery or another element of the text. Encourage students to develop claims that involve the authorial choices they feel most comfortable identifying and discussing. Struggling students often have more success with brief, image-laden narratives, while students who have more practice in this kind of reading and writing may select longer or more abstract or complex texts. Be sure the self-selected texts are appropriate, given the rigor of the task.

3. After students have drafted claims, have them work in small groups of four, using the Describing Text Templates as a lens. Students ought to be able to label each part of the claim. If the reader isn't clear about some element of the claim because it is missing, unclear, or inelegantly written, they should annotate by writing questions directly on the claim and share their feedback with the claim maker. Students should then revise claims and

incorporate them into a solid opening paragraph, using the summaries they constructed in the earlier step.

4. Have students submit the opening paragraphs so you can select samples for a whole class workshop, using the format described in the next step.

Lesson Step 9.7: Whole Class Writing Workshop

Teacher-to-Teacher Note. Busy English teachers need not spend time on detailed comments for every student early in the drafting process. Getting a handle on general strengths and needs of a class is enough on a first draft. Since many of the issues that students have with a writing assignment are common at the beginning, a whole class discussion with a couple of rich samples can save a lot of time for both students and teachers. Individual comments and student conferences will prove much more fruitful after initial revisions based on a whole group discussion of major issues. Hearing positive and constructive feedback from teachers and peers is engaging and instructive; students enjoy being the subject of discussion. Also, it is another opportunity to model and guide peer analysis of student writing, which helps students hone their workshopping skills.

1. Select a few opening paragraphs to explore in a whole class workshop. Before copying the samples of opening paragraphs, be sure to remove names. The samples should be promising (key thematic ideas, accurate use of terms, etc.) yet reveal room for improvement in key areas of summary and claim (missing parts, unclear ideas about theme, uses of jargon, etc.). By key areas I mean the areas in which most students in the class seem to be having the same kinds of problems. Your revision process should be projected, and students should record your comments on their own copies for later reference.

2. Assure students that their work with summary and claim will become the basis for an explication, and they will be revising this opening paragraph as they develop their essays. They will be learning more about the poem with each close reading and each sentence they compose about it.

3. Ask students to begin commenting on the sample by discussing the strengths of both the summaries and the claims. Focus first on what is working. Then open up the discussion for areas of improvement, especially focusing on the need for further explanation and smoother incorporation of literary terms. (This is especially problematic in the portion of the claim in which the student reveals the *choice* that will be the focus of his or her essay.) Students writing explications for the first time often use literary terms eagerly, but not always elegantly, which is why the attention to phrasing in the samples is so important.

4. After your discussion, be sure to give students enough time to make revisions on their own opening paragraphs before leaving class. Circulate to answer questions, using their claims as the basis of a mini-lesson on employing explicative language in claim making. The large claims that you talk through with students will become their models, but the talk-through that you have with individual students can be the "aha" moment for which everyone has been waiting, so make sure you meet with as many students as possible. Reserve the time for it; this is when you can call upon sacred silent writing time practices again! As you circulate or meet with students individually or in small groups, be sure each student is experiencing success in claim making. If some students' difficulties seem insurmountable, you may have to encourage them to adjust their poem selection or rethink the focus of their claim.

More Poems for Practice

"A Blessing" by James Wright (widely accessible), "The Hate Poem" by Julie Sheehan (more difficult), and "Mending Wall" by Robert Frost (challenging.) These poems work well when using agency analysis as a gateway for comprehension. Have students at lower levels of readiness identify agents and actions in "A Blessing" or another accessible poem and write a sentence or two describing the main agents of action in the poem. Then have them summarize the poem. Have on-level students read one of the poems without focusing on anything in particular and then read it again, identifying all the agents and actions, before reflecting in writing on how reading for agency changed their experience. Have advanced students describe in a paragraph how a poet manipulates agency in a section of a poem in order to support a particular idea.

More Close Reading, Performance, and Powerful Writing Ideas

Close Reading

Have students summarize the claim and supporting evidence found in the sample explication, challenging them to provide a concise but accurate description of the explicator's interpretation.

Performance

Have students collect texts from different genres and historical periods (the bigger the range, the better) that tell us something about the battle of the sexes. Have students bring in pictures, etiquette books, signs, commercials, poems, old textbooks or picture books, sociological texts, and the like, and ask, "What are some of the common themes in this ongoing battle?" Have them physicalize these texts using performance techniques from earlier lessons and create a larger performance that comments on this battle.

Artful Writing

Have students write about a time when they witnessed or took part in a conflict between two opposing forces (friend/enemy, wise self/reckless self, parent/child, etc.). As they revise original pieces, have them consider the ways in which verb choice can add a twist to an image. For example, instead of a brother "yelling," could he be "pecking"?

Curricular Debate Resolution

Gender is a destiny, an identity that cannot be escaped.

Lesson 10: Analyzing How Syntax and Sentence Variety Shape Meaning in a Poem

Teacher-to-Teacher Note. "Traveling through the Dark" by William Stafford is a difficult poem to teach. It can raise challenging questions, both literary and ethical, but it is really worth every effort readers are willing to give it. The concrete story alone is a powerful one, without any analysis. But when students apply the tools for literary analysis they have gained thus far, they will be able to explore the many artful and ideological nuances of the story. With this narrative poem, students will explore the nature of ethics and learn to account for poets' choices regarding additional aspects of verbs, sentence types, and syntax.

The writing component of the lesson focuses on the development of supporting paragraphs in explications. All the supporting paragraphs and sentences in an explication are subclaims. Using the poem itself as the organizational guide, students will learn to support the overall claims they developed in the previous lesson as they move from the beginning to the end of the poem. Paragraphs and the sentences within an explication are typically developed using mini-claims about each part of the poem (line-by-line, chunk-by-chunk, stanza-by-stanza claims). Students will also learn techniques for weaving textual supports into their sentences and paragraphs, beginning new paragraphs with each new stanza or with each meaningful chunk or part of the poem.

It may be helpful to review parts of poems at this point. Dividing a poem into parts is discussed in detail in lesson 2 (Chapter 2) on Sharon Olds's "I Go Back to May 1937." Briefly, though, the division of a poem into parts can be determined by major changes in theme, topic, time, place, speaker, subject, or tone, or even by changes in certain elements of language.

Lesson Step 10.1: Exploring Sentence Parts

1. *Frontloading Knowledge Option:* Before introducing "Traveling through the Dark," have students perform a quick-write and facilitate a small group discussion based on the following debatable resolution: Human life is more valuable than animal life. This is a provocative idea that comes up in the reading of this poem, so it is worth thinking about prior to the reading. Assure students, who will readily engage in debate on the issue, that the issues raised by this poem will help them explore that very question and will also deepen their understanding of the nature of ethics.

2. Let students know that before they read the poem, they'll review another element of verbs to help them get the most from their reading. Have students take out their Key Literary Terms for Discussing the Verb and Other Sentence Parts (handout 9.A in the appendix). Then project these two sentences:

   - The boys ate the pizza.
   - The pizza was eaten.

   Introduce the idea that just as they used other keys to exploring verbs, they will look for another important aspect of sentence construction as it relates to verbs: the active and the passive voice. Tell them that they will continue examining verbs (actions or states of being) and then looking for the agents (the performers of the actions), and that they now will look at how other parts of a sentence fall around those two essential parts. Introduce the concepts using "The boys ate the pizza" as an example. Ask two more questions:

   - What is the action of this sentence? (ate)
   - Who performed the action of eating? (the boys)

Then explain that this is an example of the active voice, a clause in which an agent is clearly responsible for the action, but that there are also sentences in which no particular agent seems to perform the action. Sometimes no agent is noted. It's just left out (passive voice).

Using the second example, "The pizza was eaten," ask students to name the action and note that no agent has performed the action. This is an example of the passive voice. I often point out that the passive voice is used in academic, scientific, political, and legal writing to create an air of authority by removing fallible human agents or, in some cases, to avoid indicating responsibility for an action. It is important to note that even when a prepositional phrase is added to the sentence (by the boys) to indicate the agent of action, the sentence itself can make grammatical sense without it. From a grammatical standpoint, the sentence proper is still constructed in the passive voice because it would still make sense even without the prepositional phrase that gives us the information about agent.

While poets rarely use the passive voice, there are other ways to manipulate syntax, as Stafford does, that allows him to avoid assigning a human agent, while maintaining the active voice. Giving agency to inanimate objects and avoiding the assignment of an agent to a particular action are tricks of the poetic trade that Stafford employs masterfully in this poem. Students will discover that he avoids assigning agency to verbs in several sentences by using the infinitive form of verbs and unusual syntax (the meaningful relationships in the order of parts of a sentence).

See handout 9.A, Key Literary Terms for Discussing the Verb and Other Sentence Parts, for important definitions and examples of technical terms used in the explication. To demonstrate the idea of syntax as an important feature in creating meaning, I use Lewis Carroll's "Jabberwocky" and have students determine the parts of speech for each of the nonsense words, illustrating that we can tell agent from action, and adjective from adverb, even without knowing the meaning of the words simply because they relate to each other in particular ways based on meaningful relationships between identifiable parts in the sentence such as articles.

3. Introduce "Traveling through the Dark" by sharing brief background information on William Stafford. He is one of America's most prolific poets. He wrote tens of thousands of poems in his lifetime and did not begin publishing them until later in his life. He lived much of his life in the western part of the United States and employed that region's imagery in much of his work, which often reveals his passion for environmental issues.

4. Have students prepare a brief impromptu performance of the poem by physicalizing the story in slow motion. Image by image, they should develop a silent, physical representation of the action that unfolds in the story.

5. Next, tell students they will have five to seven minutes to prepare a performance of the poem that illustrates the emotional drama the speaker undergoes. Every member of the group must speak some part of it, and every member of the group must be part of the visual performance. To facilitate everyone's participation, have students deploy single, dual, and choral (whole group) voices during their presentation at some point in the performance. Have them pay special attention to changes in tone and consider how these changes correspond with other elements of the text such as imagery, syntax, and the like.

Vocal representations of the drama are the desired product. To begin thinking about vocalizing the text, ask students to recall the possible antecedent scenarios for this utterance. As you circulate like a director, use the following questions to prompt a range of presentations. Be sure to note that you don't necessarily have evidence to suggest that the speaker is the poet or that the speaker is male, but for ease of discussing it, we can refer to the speaker as *he*:

- What do you imagine about the speaking situation? Is the speaker telling this story casually to an old friend? Confessing it to his son or daughter?
- How does the emotional reliving of this moment sound coming out of the speaker's mouth?
- How does the speaker feel about what he has done?
- What lesson or commentary about being human might the speaker want to impart to this audience in telling this story?

6. Have students share performances; then wrap up the impromptu performances by asking students to share the gist of the poem.

Lesson Step 10.2: Analyzing Active and Passive Voice

1. After discussing the gist of the poem, model an annotation that focuses on labeling sentences according to the speaker's use of verbs. With students, go line by line, indicating when the speaker assigns a particular agent to an action and when the agent is withheld. Though voice is always active, he often avoids assigning responsibility to a particular agent. Model an analysis using the first stanza.

   I am going to underline the verbs (action words or verbs of being) first.

   Have students assist ("found," "is," "roll," "is," "swerve," "make").

   Now I am going to circle agents or who is doing each of the actions.

   Have students assist ("I").

   "I" is the only agent named in the first stanza. It is striking to me that there were all these action words, but no one seems to be doing them in several cases where the infinitive is used. Why might that be?

2. Ask students to consider how the use of the infinitive, which allows the speaker to avoid assigning an agent, affects the meaning of the sentence by having them rewrite several sentences with an agent. Begin with the last two lines of the first stanza, where there are three examples with no particular agent being assigned: "It is usually best to roll them into the canyon: / that road is narrow; to swerve might make more dead."

Next, have students insert possible agents for the verbs "roll," "swerve," and "make." Write sample sentences on the board. Then ask how each possible rewrite raises new issues in this ethical dilemma. Look through the rest of the poem as a class, discussing how the speaker manipulates agency in this way.

3. Have students continue on their own in small groups, underlining every verb and circling the agent or the owner of each action (not just the main verb of the sentence, but each image, every line).

4. As you circulate, model Key Literary Terms for Discussing Verbs and Other Sentence Parts (handout 9.A) as well as other key terms. Be sure each individual student has success in identifying verbs and their agents. Like agency, being able to talk with students about how writers employ verbs is useful for writers conferences, student workshops, and critical discussions of text. Model claim statements that fit the Describing Text Template orally, and prompt students to use textual evidence in their discussions with each other. They should challenge each other to defend claims early on at this point.

5. Project the entire text and have students share summaries of the poem. Then complete a whole class annotation.

6. As students discuss the implications of Stafford's choices, they should consider the reasons why the speaker might be inclined to use this unusual syntax. Compare, for example, the lack of agents in the first stanza with the use of agents in stanza two. What might account for the change? Students may discuss the nature of ethical dilemmas, which involve conflicts between the general rule (it is ethical that an animal life is sacrificed for human life when one has no other choice) and certain crisis situations where particular forces beyond our control make the general rule seem inapplicable or less clearly right (unborn fawn on the roadside.)

7. Before wrapping up the discussion, students should write individual answers to the following questions and share their responses, so they can practice claim making in writing and aloud.

   ■ What does the technique of moving from the suppression of agents to the clear assignment of agency reveal about the speaker's perception of his own role in this situation?

   ■ How does the speaker's perception of the situation change from the beginning to the end of the poem?

   ■ What commentary does Stafford seem to be making about the nature of ethical decision making in this poem?

   ■ What techniques does Stafford use to make his commentary on ethical decision making through the form of a poem?

Lesson Step 10.3: Using Textual Evidence to Develop Paragraphs in an Explication

Teacher-to-Teacher Note. Remember: all the supporting paragraphs and sentences in an explication are subclaims. An explication walks readers through each part of the poem—in some cases, every line, sentence, and stanza—from the beginning to the end, using many subclaims that support the large claim. In this step, students will use the sample explication of "Traveling through the Dark," found as handout 10.A in the appendix, to explore mini-claims at work.

1. Have students read through the sample explication, identifying its overall claim and discussing its parts using the Describing Text Templates (handout 9.D) and the process found in the previous lesson. Then have them note mini-claims that are made throughout the rest of the essay. Have them look for the choice maker, verbs, choice (word, technique, image, etc.), associated meanings, and interpreted meanings. Students may actually record and label the parts as in the previous step.

    Again, the associated meanings and interpreted meanings are those text-to-self, text-to-text, and text-to-world connections that allow poets to rely on commonly shared experiences to convey meaning to readers. Sometimes they are familiar tropes such as a river or a road that suggest a metaphorical journey, while other times they are details that reveal things without saying them explicitly, like the word "purred" in the Stafford poem, which suggests comfort and warmth.

2. Have students read through the sample explication again to see how explicators communicate the entire poem, without copying the entire poem onto the page, noting sentences that introduce, explain, summarize, or weave in text from the poem. Have them highlight or underline examples of direct quotations, summary, paraphrase, and description and label them as such.

3. In a large group debrief of this exercise ask students, "How does the writer make use of the text in the argument?" In other words, how else other than direct quotation does the writer use the text to support the explication? Have students point to specific examples of other ways (summary, paraphrase, description) in which text may be used to support an argument.

4. After discussing the claims and the use of textual evidence, have students examine the way paragraphs are broken. Have students individually determine the reasons why the writer moves from one paragraph to another; then have them share in a small or large group closing discussion. Have them take a moment to analyze transitions from one paragraph to the next by asking, "What is the reason for a new paragraph? What words and phrases are used to make the transition from one paragraph to another?"

Students should note paragraphs are organized around key developments in the poem, and since the poem is a narrative, each new development coincides with an event in this brief story.

5. If they haven't done so already, have students return to work with their selected poems (from the summary and claim exercise) and complete their original explication drafts, paying special attention to constructing subclaims, incorporating a variety of textual evidence, and determining paragraph boundaries. (Be sure to share a rubric. See the Explication Rubric, handout 9.F in the appendix, before students begin drafting. *Please note:* The rubric represents an atomistic approach to evaluating writing, rather than a holistic approach. It also doesn't tend to the nuances of a writer's command over language, originality, or depth of thought. A more holistic rubric can be provided at various points along the way to describe the strengths and areas for revision before final grading rubrics are provided. Consider it a starting point, rather than an end-all, be-all description of good explicative writing.)

Lesson Step 10.4: Whole Class and Small Group Explication Workshops and Individual Student Conferences

Teacher-to-Teacher Note. The focus of the first whole class explication workshop is to find errors of omission. In other words, this workshop focuses on finding interpretations that lack the accompanying explanation to help readers understand how explicators reached their conclusions. Younger writers sometimes think everyone will see the text exactly as they do. Through this process, students become more adept at finding the omissions on their own and revising them out with more explanation and more evidence. The most important work in this process is helping students spell out their thinking. I have found that adolescents share original and brilliant interpreted meanings but often have trouble articulating what led to the interpretation. Students who have not written academic arguments before are not always aware of the burden of evidence, so now is the time for peers to focus on coaching each other to incorporate textual evidence and to guide an audience's interpretation of it.

Another major issue in early drafts will be the muddled paragraphing. This is the moment at which we wonder why we ever disparaged the five-paragraph essay with the neat little three-point claim. We have to face this disorder with courage, recover our senses, and remember that the students have done amazing analytical thinking and are saying really smart things, even if those things are coming out a bit jumbled up. The main purpose of this first explication is to get students thinking deeply about the construction of a text and developing fluency in describing text. Students will focus on revising their explications with peers over the next two lessons (more articulate sentences, then more organized paragraphs).

1. Before or after completing an initial peer workshop, using the Explication Workshop handout (handout 10.B in the appendix), have students submit drafts of an entire explication and sort through them looking for rich student samples to illustrate one or two strengths and main areas of concern. Make copies after removing student names and project them for the whole class to see.

2. A good sample should illustrate promise and a need for improvement that is common among many other students (this may range from organizing a paragraph to constructing a claim). At this stage, I often wish for a rubber stamp that says: "The ideas in this paragraph seem to relate to the same part of the poem, but I am not sure on what the paragraph is focused. Maybe you need a good topic sentence that tells me what development this part of the poem is describing." Or "I sort of understand what you mean, but I need to see more explanation and more support from the text to understand how you arrived at this interesting idea." Or "What do you mean by _____?" Or "How do the specifics of the text lead you to this association, which is really interesting?"

3. Begin, as always, by looking at what is working, asking students to point out the strengths of a student sample. Then focus your questions, comments, and sample revision work on a single area of concern that applies to the majority of the class or to a small group with whom you are working. Students should record comments and suggestions for revisions on the sample.

4. Provide "my paper" time after each sample paper revision activity in the whole class workshop so students have time to examine and revise their papers in light of each aspect of revision you have highlighted.

5. After two rounds of whole class workshopping—three at most—have students reexamine their own explications and revise. Again honor the student drafts with class time, so that students can consult you during this complex process.

6. Next, have students workshop their best independent drafts in pairs or small groups if time allows for more than one reader to workshop the paper. The first workshop and perhaps the second should be focused on making sense of good thematic ideas. Share the questions found on the Explication Workshop handout, and make sure students read silently and write in complete sentences on their partner's paper before discussing it with the writer. This is where the creative writing workshop training comes into play. Students will need both their explications and copies of their poem to share with peers.

7. Repeat student workshops several times if necessary, having students revise in between while you meet with individual stu-

dents. The focus of remaining workshops ought to be on evidence, organization, elegance, and, finally, conventions. Students should be pushing each other to write evidence-filled paragraphs that support the larger claim using just the facts, all the facts, and nothing but the facts of the poem.

Individual teacher-student conferences using the precise vocabulary you and your students now share are most fruitful at this stage. Your familiarity with the original draft, along with a focus on key areas for development, makes for efficient conferencing. As we all know, a seven- to ten-minute conference with each student on a brief essay can make all the difference in writing instruction, moving everyone forward in a common direction, while accommodating differences in terms of pace and mastery levels. Plan ahead for in-class and out-of-class conference time at this crucial stage, if possible. (See Rick Wormeli's work 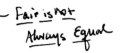 on differentiating assessment.) While this may be impossible to do regularly, we should attempt to build in regular conference time each semester.

8. Have students complete final revisions of their explications before submitting them for evaluation.

More Poems for Practice

"At the Un-National Monument along the Canadian Border," "A Ritual to Read to Each Other," and "At the Bomb Testing Site" are accessible poems by William Stafford that lend themselves to further exploration of the themes and techniques in "Traveling through the Dark." Focusing on a single author and exploring common themes deepens a reader's understanding of all of the writer's poems. Have students at lower levels of readiness work with the poem they selected for their explication project to analyze agency and write a brief reflection of how reading the poem through that lens had an impact on their understanding of the poem. Have on-level students select a few excerpts of the poem about which they are writing and describe the impact of a poet's selection of a particular agent of action in a particular image, phrase, or sentence on a particular idea. In addition to the on-level task, have advanced students research and read several pieces of criticism about their poem or poet and carefully summarize the other writer's ideas.

More Close Reading, Performance, and Powerful Writing Ideas

Close Reading

Using the Describing Text Template, have students develop a claim about the poetry of William Stafford and support it with brief explicative paragraphs on a group of poems.

Performance

This poem is so full of drama that it is really a wonderful piece for recitation. Encourage students to prepare a recitation of this poem or another of Stafford's poems using the sample recitation assignment from lesson 4. Alternatively, have students physicalize a range of nature poetry in an ensemble until a clear theme about nature emerges to guide a performance based on the title "The Poet Speaks of the Natural World."

Artful Writing

Have students write about a moment in which they had to make a difficult choice; then have them take a close look at their verbs, revising a sentence written in the active voice to passive, or vice versa, to determine the impact of these choices on syntax and ultimately tone. If they want to go the next step further, they might even try one of Stafford's infinitive tricks!

Curricular Debate Resolution

Resolved: The speaker in the poem "Traveling through the Dark" is certain he has done the right thing by the end of the poem. See lesson step 9.2 for ad hoc debate instructions, through which students can conduct mini-debates based upon this resolution.

Lesson 11: Understanding How Poets Create Varying Speech Acts within Sentences and Lines

Teacher-to-Teacher Note. In this lesson, students will explore the concept of speech act, that is, the ways in which we perform actions with our words. Leading students in this way through Walt Whitman's "Beat! Beat! Drums!" allows them to practice asking another set of questions that will help them get the gist of a text, delve into close reading, and ultimately create better arguments about texts.

Like the preceding lesson in this chapter involving "Traveling through the Dark," the second half of the lesson is devoted to developing more powerful supporting paragraphs for their original explications. Students will learn to strengthen these evidence-filled paragraphs by selecting more precise verbs for describing the actions and ideas within a text and for describing a writer's choices in the creation of a text. They will also revisit paragraph organization.

Lesson Step 11.1: Introducing Speech Act

1. *Frontloading Knowledge Option:* Before introducing the poem, have students perform a quick-write on the following question: "Is it

ethical for nations to recruit their young to fight wars?" After students have had an opportunity to discuss the issue, segue into your introduction of the poem by letting students know that "Beat! Beat! Drums!" was written, published, and revised several times during the course of the Civil War before becoming part of Walt Whitman's book *Drum Taps* (1865). If students need more background information about the American Civil War, PBS has wonderful documentary footage and teaching resources related to Whitman in Ken Burns's series *The Civil War.*

2. Before introducing the poem, explain that through words, humans perform actions. We issue orders, offer explanations, say prayers, make claims, and apologize; we even perform all sorts of legal actions, including committing to marriage or agreeing to tell the truth under oath! To introduce the concept of speech act, I have students consider one-word sentences. I project the following:

   - Right?
   - Right.
   - Go?
   - Go!

   Then I have student volunteers say these four illustrative examples aloud.

   As students intone these sentences, they can hear how the very same words can mean entirely different things depending upon the speech act they are intended to perform. Ask students to consider what action each of these one-word sentences performs: "Right?" seeks confirmation or agreement. "Right" affirms. "Go?" asks a question. "Go!" issues a command. In using a question mark as opposed to the period, for example, the word "Right?" is really a complete sentence that asks "Do you agree?" or "Am I correct?" These examples show how intonation, especially in spoken text, has as much to do with conveying meaning as the semantic meaning of the words themselves. Explain to students that just like individual lines within a poem, entire poems have to be considered in terms of speech acts as well. The genre of a poem can take the form of an elegy, a prayer, a definition, and so on.

3. In written text, we often use punctuation, such as a question mark, to guide a reader's interpretation of the intended speech act. But poetry, like the sheet music of a great symphony, sometimes offers itself to many valid interpretations and may be intoned differently by each reader depending upon their interpretation. As poets craft their words, they are mindful of the notion of speech act; sometimes they cue readers about how to intone a sentence for a particular performative effect, and sometimes their cues allow us to explore a doubleness or tripleness that challenges readers to examine the subtle complexities of an idea. (Think back to

the Sir Thomas Wyatt poem in which the speaker's lover asks, "Dear heart, how like you this?" It can be read as two distinctly different questions: "Do you like what I'm doing?" or "How do you like being treated this way?") Indeed, the doubleness or tripleness of a line's meaning is often part of a poem's genius. This key element differentiates literature from other kinds of writing. Exploring multiple possibilities for speech act is yet another way to investigate the speaker's attitude toward the subject or to explore a poem's tone and how tone might shape the way the poem is spoken aloud.

4. As always, sharing a little background about the poet gives students something to grab onto and sometimes provides an interesting hook. Here is how I introduce Whitman's poem:

> Walt Whitman is widely considered the father of modern American poetry. He celebrated the themes of diversity, individuality, and freedom through images and words from everyday American life. His work in the nineteenth century established a uniquely American voice among the world's great poets. His reach into the twenty-first century and beyond affirms his influence as a master and as an innovator. The following poem is a work composed at the beginning of the American Civil War, a war he thought was just and necessary, and in which several of his own brothers fought.

> Whitman covered the war as a journalist and volunteered in field hospitals, witnessing the horrors of war firsthand. Published in *Drum Taps* (1865), this "recruitment poem," as many scholars read it, gives insight into Whitman's initial belief in the Union's cause—saving the republic. Contemporary readers may see it differently, which, incidentally, raises interesting questions about the construction of the poem itself. Since the subject is war, it is important to contract with students about being sensitive to the fact that members of their own learning community may have very close ties to those currently serving in the armed forces around the globe today. It is a provocative issue.

5. In small groups, have students think aloud as they read the poem, applying the strategies from previous lessons: visualization, identifying antecedent scenarios and SOAPSTone, dividing the poem into parts, and paraphrasing. As their discussions unfold, some students may see this as an antiwar poem, in which a speaker ironically issues commands yet shows in vivid detail the destructive effects of war on civil society; others will argue the poem is an exuberant plea to recruit fighters for a just war.

6. After a large group debrief of their initial findings, have students explore competing interpretations using the technique of exploring line break, which was introduced in lesson 5 in Chapter 3. The technique involves looking at the text as a set of *sentences*,

then as set of *lines*, separate units of meaning distinct from the sentences of which they are a part. Poets play with enjambment, allowing readers to take away one meaning from a line and a different meaning when that line is read as part of a sentence. Then, as an example, look at the last line of the first stanza. "So fierce you whirr and pound you drums—so shrill you bugles blow."

Read the whole stanza aloud. Point to the last lines and ask, "Is that last line an order or an accusation?" To heighten their awareness of both possibilities, have a volunteer say that particular line out loud as an *order* from the commander of the bugles and drums. Then have a volunteer say it aloud as if it were an *accusation* against the destructive drums and bugles, coming from someone who is pleading to stop the war. As part of the sentence this line must be spoken as a *command*, where "so" might be replaced with the word *therefore*. In this scenario, the speaker is arguing that the war is worth fighting (to end slavery, to save the union, etc.) and is worth any amount of sacrifice; therefore, people cannot carry on with their everyday lives. Taken as a separate unit of meaning, however, this *line* could be an *accusation* that explains the result of these deafening drums. The drums of war are the ruin of everyday living. This *line* could be spoken as an answer to the question "What is the cause of this horror?" The word "so" would be an adverb, describing the degree of fierceness with which the drum is whirring and pounding.

7. To deepen student interest about whether this can only be read as a recruitment poem or if it is also possible to read it as an antiwar poem, have students take a close look at the role of line break in determining speech act. Explain that Whitman wrote the poem early on in the war, genuinely believing that the war was just, but by the date of its publication in book form, Whitman's views on the war may have been tempered by the horrors he witnessed. He spent a great deal of time volunteering in field hospitals, where wounded soldiers suffered. The bloody conflict took a toll on his family and on hundreds of thousands of others. *Drum Taps* in many ways is a chronicle of changing sentiments about the war, revealed through the American poetic lens.

Have students analyze both possibilities by having them label each *sentence* according to the type of speech act the speaker is performing. Then look at each *line* separately and consider other possible speech acts that each line might be performing. In small groups, readers should experiment with different readings aloud, always asking, "What is the speaker doing here? What action is the speaker performing with words?"

For example, is he or she dispensing a command, making a plea, asking a question, or explaining a cause and effect relationship? As students practice this strategy, it is useful to have them type out or write out the entire poem as a series of sentences and as a series of self-contained lines to explore the difference between line and sentence meaning. Above all, it is essential that they practice saying each line aloud according to the speaker's intention.

8. Bring students back together to share their findings. Project the text and label the speech act line by line and then sentence by sentence before returning to the question of whether this should be read as a recruitment poem or as an antiwar poem. Ultimately, the question relates to the overall speech act of the text. Ask students, "Is the text a recruitment poem or an antiwar poem? What is the overall speech act here?"

Optional Lesson Step: Getting Ready to Recite "Beat! Beat! Drums!"

Teacher-to-Teacher Note. The question of whether we ought to read it as a recruitment poem or an antiwar poem is an excellent subject for academic debate and also an excellent opportunity for students to present competing interpretations through dueling recitations. Have students review the guide in handout 11.A and prepare full-blown recitations or simple ad hoc staged readings.

1. Give students time to prepare presentations and share them in class. After sharing recitations, have students discuss their final interpretations based on the question "Is this a recruitment poem or an antiwar poem, or can it be both?"

2. To wrap up, students might want to entertain questions about the role of author or artist intention versus audience interpretation. "Who ought to have authority over our understanding of a poem—the poet, the poem, or the reader? If a reader interprets a poem differently than an author intended, is that okay? Can a poem still be considered a good poem if this happens? What contextual factors may cause readers to interpret differently? Can a number of conflicting interpretations of a poem be valid?"

Optional Lesson Step: Ad Hoc Debates

Rather than or in addition to the dueling recitation approach, students may debate a resolution about the poem using the ad hoc debate format found in lesson step 9.2. The resolution I recommend for "Beat! Beat! Drums!" is "Whitman's speaker is being ironic, not vehement, when he encourages people to go to war."

Lesson Step 11.2: Analyzing Another Sample Explication

1. Explain that just like writers of imaginative texts (poetry, drama, and fiction), strong academic writers are very conscious of their verb choices. A good verb choice can be a great workhorse, accomplishing many tasks at once. Follow the steps below to

    illustrate this concept as you share and review student handout 11.B, a sample explication of "Beat! Beat! Drums!"

2. Remind students that academic writers are constantly making arguments as they summarize and describe. In fact, as the sample sentences from the Sir Thomas Wyatt explication (handout 9.C) show, the explicator often describes, summarizes, and argues all at once. The writer describes his or her overall interpretation of the poem in his or her large claim, but the heart of the supporting argument lies in the verbs that make up sentences throughout the explication. Have students read the Sample Explication of "Beat! Beat! Drums!" and mark at least three sentences with a heart (agreed or good point), a question mark (disagreed or must discuss), or a check mark (disagree).

3. In small groups, have students summarize the large claim. Then, in a whole class debrief, share their findings and additional comments and questions about the explication.

4. Next, have students independently reread the first paragraph or two, circling the verbs and underlining agents as they read. Have students note how an explicator gives agency to the *writer's choice*, while at other times it is the *speaker* or the *text* itself that seems to perform an action. Have students find an example of where the explicator assigns responsibility for an action to the following agents: the poet, the speaker, a literary device (image, metaphor, simile, etc.), or a mark of punctuation. In the next step, students will revise the explications they have been crafting using this heightened consciousness of how one describes a text. (Additional teaching notes for leading students through a revision focused on agency in explicative writing are included with handout 11.B in the appendix.)

Lesson Step 11.3: Revising through an Examination of Agency and Verb Choice

Teacher-to-Teacher Note. Since jumbling may still be a challenge for some students, work with sentence-level revisions may be targeted at the topic sentences that set the stage for each new paragraph. If students spend time on refining those topic sentences, they will have a better time of focusing their evidence throughout the paragraph as well.

1. Distribute and review the Verbs for Describing Texts handout (11.C in the appendix), which was, incidentally, compiled by my students from professional pieces of literary analysis. As an extension to this exercise, you might have students research professional explications of poems and create their own lists of verbs. (Sources designed for high school and undergraduate courses—such as *Poetry Criticism*, *The Explicator*, *Contemporary Literary Criticism*, and the like—are great for this fruitful assignment.)

2. Begin the revision process by modeling verb choice revision with a few sample student paragraphs. Project and distribute copies of the samples. Ideally, these models should offer themselves to the possibility of revision through agency and verb choice. Lead students through an examination of sample student sentences and ask students to make suggestions, using the lists, for more exact or more useful verbs. Be sure suggestions are substantiated as to why one verb accomplishes more than another in terms of the claim. See Presentation of Revision Homework (teaching aid 1 in the appendix) and Before and After: Workshopping with Templates and Revising Verb Choice (teaching aid 2) for useful examples.

3. Working in small groups, students should revise a sentence or two from their own paragraphs by revising their choice of agent. For example, instead of beginning a sentence with "The poet suggested," it would be more accurate to say, "The speaker suggested," or "The poet's choice indicated," or something similarly precise. Have students use the Verbs for Describing Text handout and select a few verbs for revision from their own writing. Indicate that the precision of the verb is key to good explicative writing. Circulate and conduct mini-conferences as students work in small groups. This is also a good time to ensure that the paragraphs are focused on a clear interpretive claim and that they are well supported.

4. It is time to collect these well-wrought explications and evaluate them. As you evaluate, I encourage you to reward the strengths of each explication, especially at the sentence level. The lessons have focused on developing student fluency with claims and subclaims, much more than they have focused on paragraphing and organization, so the evaluations ought to reflect that focus as well. The culminating explication in the next lesson will allow you to reinforce all of those values and to zero in on paragraphing as well.

More Poems for Practice

"Dulce Et Decorum Est" by Wilfred Owen (somewhat difficult) and "Here, Bullet" by Brian Turner (fairly accessible) are war poems that also open up in interesting ways when entered through an analysis of speech act, especially when analyzed out loud with consideration to line break. "The March into Virginia Ending in the First Manassas" (July 1861) and "Shiloh" (April 1862) by Herman Melville are challenging but wonderful poems for exploring changing speech acts, and they serve as contemporary counterpoints to Whitman's work in some ways. Students at lower levels of readiness should be writing paragraphs about poems and researching and reading explications just like everyone else. Rather than steering students into difficult scholarly texts, select poems and accompanying readings from the periodical *Poetry for Students* and other sources designed specifically for younger readers. Whether students are on their way, on level, or advanced, have them read and summarize a secondary piece of writing about a poem, after annotating key features of explications including claims, subclaims (topic sentences and supporting sentences,) paragraph breaks, and verb choice. Advanced students should be asked to incorporate information from secondary sources into their paragraphs.

More Close Reading, Performance, and Powerful Writing Ideas

Close Reading

Students can research "Beat! Beat! Drums!" and other poems from Whitman's *Drum Taps* and find model explications for these poems. They can even see changes from various editions. Students can then develop a paper discussing the influence of the Civil War on Whitman's poetry. The book's publication history is especially interesting.

Performance

Have students find and develop other texts (poems, speeches, narratives, laws, proclamations, tweets, etc.), especially those from the era of the Civil War, and use them to develop a performance that helps an audience explore different perspectives on the Civil War and its legacies in contemporary global life. I have recently worked with a number of teachers who have connected Whitman's poem to bullying and youth violence.

Artful Writing

Have students write a script made of found text that illuminate the terms *civil* and *war*.

Curricular Debate Topic

Herman Melville wrote the poem "The March into Virginia Ending in the First Manassas," in which he, like Whitman, comments on the boys and men recruited to fight the Civil War. Using "Beat! Beat! Drums!" and Melville's poem, have students engage in mini-debates on the following resolutions:

- Melville's poem expresses the view that recruiting young men to fight a war is wrong.

■ Whitman's poem expresses the view that recruiting young men
or anyone else to fight a war is sometimes just and necessary.

Lesson 12: Analyzing How the Parts Reflect the Whole

Teacher-to-Teacher Note. Students have had a lot of practice reading poems closely with their peers and developing an explication with a lot of
support. Now it is time for them to try it more independently. The focus
of this last lesson in close reading is on exploring thematic unity in the
poem. It is time for students to employ all of the close reading strategies
they've been practicing in order to discover how all the big and little
parts of a great poem are united by thematic coherency. Students may
end up focusing on the revelations of only a few close reading strategies
as they draft an explication, but they should explore 360 degrees of the
poem before determining the focus of their claim, so I encourage teachers
to have students employ those performance and imitation strategies as
they prepare their final projects.

While the final project is ultimately a nontraditional academic product, I believe that writing a text about a text is another way to understand
it, a way to process one's learning as a result of using other approaches.
Secondly, if your students are like mine, they have gotten pretty good at
noticing interesting things and making great claims, but the things can get
a bit jumbled up in their explications. The writing portion of this lesson
is focused on paragraph coherency and is the final step.

Unlike other lessons, in which the teacher presented a very specific
entrée into the poem, students should be challenged to construct and
represent the poem's meaning independently. (Remember? I do it, we
do it together, you do it together, you do it alone.) With the Lorna Dee
Cervantes poem they are about to explore, students will examine the
ways in which each aspect of three major elements of the poem (imagery,
form, and language) contribute to the theme. After modeling this, you
will challenge students to find that coherency in a poem of their choice.

At the end of the 360-degree tour, I celebrate all modes of representing meaning (group performance, recitation, imitation, multimedia, art,
etc.) because they can be dazzling experiences that help everyone understand why poetry as an art form has remained one of the most important
parts of all human cultures! The sky is the limit in terms of the products
students share in representing the meaning of the poems they select.

However, the college prep English teacher in me also requires a
written explication, not because it is better than other ways of representing
meaning, but because it is an important route to constructing meaning,

and because it is the one that is rewarded most in academia. While this explication can simply be graded like their other formal essays, students may elect to use it as part of a performance-oriented culminating project (program text for a performance, a placard to accompany a painting, an opening argument in a debate, etc.) Students can collaborate with you to devise a rubric for evaluating their independent projects. For reliable sources of the poem's text see "Additional Resources for Chapter 4."

Lesson Step 12.1: Independent Study Reflection

Before sending students off with their poetic licenses in hand, it is important for them to reflect upon what they have learned about reading texts. This abbreviated independent study of Lorna Dee Cervantes's 1998 poem "Freeway 280" will give students an opportunity to reflect metacognitively on their own reading strategies and remind them of the strategies they now have in their toolbox for approaching a poem of their choice.

1. *Frontloading Knowledge Option:* Share the following background on Lorna Dee Cervantes, one of the most critically acclaimed poets of our time.

   Born in San Francisco, California, in 1954, Lorna Dee Cervantes is one of America's most prominent Chicana poets. In her work, she explores the impact of race, gender, culture, and economics on individuals and their communities. In her first book of poetry, *Emplumada*, she explored Chicana identity in poems such as "Freeway 280." Many of the works in the collection, written in English, contain untranslated Spanish words. In her next two books of poetry, she continues to focus on the struggles and triumphs of Chicana women, while examining everyday social injustices and the consequences of political and social radicalism.

   (If students are not aware of California's acquisition of Mexican territory, you may want to share some brief background about the Treaty of Guadalupe Hidalgo, 1848.)

2. Let students know that the poem "Freeway 280" adds a new level of challenge for readers in that it incorporates another language, Spanish. If necessary, provide students with a glossary of Spanish terms found in the poem. English language learners and bilingual students may readily understand the use of dual languages, while others may wonder why the poet chose to write in both, rather than one. (The question of why she uses dual languages in this particular poem is a wonderful opening for the students to begin their study.)

3. Have each student work independently and silently, employing as many of the close reading strategies as possible to make sense

of and make meaning of the text. You may want to review the focus of each step of the 360-degree tour (visualization; think-alouds; antecedent scenario analysis; division into parts; genre analysis; paraphrase; SOAPStone; read-aloud; form and language analysis—genre, sonic patterns, allusion, stanzaic forms; agency analysis; speech act analysis; and sentence analysis).

4. After students have had plenty of time to work with the poem, examining the imagery, form, verbs, and sentences, have each student write complete sentences as they answer the Independent Study Reflection questions in handout 12.A.

5. Using students' written responses to the close reading activity, facilitate a large group discussion of the poem, in which the speaker explores tensions in her bicultural, bilingual identity. Ask students to discuss the ways in which the speaker represents her struggle to live in California as a Latina, often feeling neither fully Mexican nor fully American. Have students trace the aspects of the poem that reveal her inner debate, as she struggles to determine how to proceed as a member of either, neither, or both of her larger cultural communities. Have students share summaries and claims as a whole group.

6. Following their discussion of the poem, ask students to write their reflections on their own process of constructing meaning. Ask, "Did you notice a particularly useful strategy among those you've tried? Did you have any surprising results?"

7. Collect these reflections and use the data to inform your instruction as you plan additional textual analysis units.

Lesson Step 12.2: Examining the Function of Strong Topic Sentences in an Explication

Teacher-to-Teacher Note. Let students know that while the focus of previous lessons was on constructing the meaning of a poem and describing it to an audience, students will be challenged to hone their organizational skills within the context of explicative writing. This lesson is a paragraphing lesson that places special attention on the function of a topic sentence in transitioning from one part to another.

1. Point out that strong explications divide the poems into parts, either based on stanza breaks or on other developments in the poem, such as events in a narrative, changes in imagery, and so on (see lesson 2 in Chapter 1 and lesson 2 in chapter 4). As in any form of prose, paragraphs are guided by topic sentences, the subclaim that connects parts of the explication back to the larger claim and guides the development of a particular idea, which is then supported by other subclaims. Remember, the way one divides the poem into parts varies. A sonnet is often discussed quatrain by quatrain; other poems are discussed stanza by stanza. Others,

such as Stafford's "Traveling through the Dark," are divided in terms of the emotional developments of the poem. Point out that while all the sentences make claims of some sort, larger claims and subclaims serve different purposes in an explication.

2. If students find the task of developing their own topic sentences too challenging in this abbreviated activity, the same activity on paragraph coherency can be scaffolded with the topic sentences provided in optional handout 12.B, Explication Outline. Otherwise, follow the steps below.

3. Ask students how they divided the Cervantes poem in their independent reading.

4. After you have discussed possible divisions, have students work in small groups and develop a large claim and several topic sentences for supporting paragraphs in an explication.

5. After selecting a few strong sample topic sentence subclaims, have students develop supporting sentences for a single topic sentence. Give students ten to fifteen minutes to complete the paragraph individually, as you circulate to answer questions.

6. Students should perform a quick-write, reflecting on their own strengths and challenges in independent analysis and explication writing before sharing with others and revising.

Lesson Step 12.3: Evaluating Student Writing for Paragraph Coherency

1. Have students evaluate Sample Student Explications, handout 12.C in the appendix.

2. Lead students through a reading of the sample explication. Ask students to engage with it as they have with the work of their own peers and professional samples, noting what they like or agree with and what they disagree with or would like to discuss. Ask students, "What are the strengths of this piece? What might help this writer make this explication better?" Gather student suggestions and share the sample with comments to find similarities and differences between the teacher's comments and their own. Have students read the next revision, pointing out that this is a *next* draft, not a final draft. Pay close attention to the last two paragraphs, especially the before and after changes in paragraph organization.

   Note the topic sentences the sample writer uses to introduce the final developments of the poem and the ways in which each detail discussed within the paragraph serves as an example of the larger paragraph idea. Challenge students to consider how topic sentences in early paragraphs could be revised to serve the same purpose. In small groups, have students revise another of the paragraphs.

3. After exploring the student sample, have students reflect on the paragraphs they wrote about the Cervantes poem. Have them revise for strong, focused topic sentences and additional evidence before submitting their paragraphs for evaluation. Let students know that in their next explication, more attention will be paid to the role of topic sentences as transitional tools throughout the larger essay and as organizational tools that bring coherency to paragraphs.

Lesson Step 12.4: Selecting a Poem and a Product for the Identity Project

1. Have students find a poem they would like to study, but let students know that in addition to writing an explication, they will select a product to represent the meaning of the poem of their choice. While some students may choose to continue work with the Cervantes poem, others may be interested in making text-to-text connections with another piece that addresses the theme of identity, or perhaps selecting a piece they have already studied. The sky is the limit.

2. After students have had time to complete initial close reading work with their poems, conduct a whole class brainstorming session that begins by asking students to think of ways to represent their understanding of poems in addition to explication. They are to imagine that anything is possible, from a multimedia presentation to a painting. They may use the suggested activities at the end of each lesson as a source of creative writing and performance ideas, but students generally have no difficulty thinking about creative ways to represent ideas on their own.

3. Have students select a product that will spring from their work on the poem of their choice. If multiple students select the same project, allow them to work collaboratively if they choose. For example, if three students want to recite poems about identity, allow them to put the show together as a coherent group, using perhaps a common physical vocabulary, costumes, a thematically significant setting, a title, and other details. Conference with students to be sure that they select texts and projects that can reasonably be executed in the allotted time and can be shared with a public audience in some way.

4. Have students develop a timeline for checking progress on their performance-based assessment products and accompanying explications. Later, develop a timeline for the final show. If you plan to assign a grade, students should collaborate with you to determine the unique evaluation criteria for their piece.

More Poems for Practice

Other poems that explore identity themes: "won't you celebrate with me" by Lucille Clifton, "Part for the Whole" by Robert Francis, "Blood" by Naomi Shihab Nye, "Barbie Doll" by Marge Piercy, "I'm Nobody! Who Are You?" by Emily Dickinson. All of these poems can work on a number of levels and are accessible to most high school readers.

More Close Reading, Performance, and Powerful Writing Ideas

Close Reading

While extensions of this analytical work are endless, a research paper based on an author study or a particular theme, period, or genre is the most natural extension for this work at all levels of readiness. Alternatively, to reinforce the usefulness of these close reading strategies across genres, have students continue to practice applying their textual power (all the close reading strategies they have learned) to short stories, speeches, and newspaper articles.

Performance

Have students practice the close reading and performance strategies they've learned on a play or adapt a longer poem for the stage. Excerpts from a longer piece—*Metamorphosis* by Ovid, *Don Juan* (Canto V) by Lord Byron, and *Rime of the Ancient Mariner* by Samuel Taylor Coleridge are wonderful longer texts to consider for performance. Collections by an author will work too: Walt Whitman's *Drum Taps* and Gwendolyn Brooks's *A Street in Bronzeville* are ripe for this sort of work.

Artful Writing

Six-line scenes for a brief dramatic dialogue are a great starting point for a young dramatist with newly refined poetic skills. Start with two characters and create a brief scene in six lines. The length of the lines doesn't matter, but the scene cannot be longer than six lines.

Curricular Debate Topic

To be successful and happy in a multicultural America, a person's ethnic identity has to be shed.

Additional Resources for Chapter 4

Verbs and Other Sentence Parts

- Strunk and White's *The Elements of Style* is the classic resource for concise and accessible definitions and examples of all aspects of convention in English.

- Online sources such as OWL at Purdue (http://owl.english.purdue.edu/) and many lessons on the ReadWriteThink website (http://www.readwritethink.org/http://www.mozilla.org/thunderbird/) offer helpful lessons and handouts for reviewing grammar and other elements of language.

Academic Arguments, Composition, and Explication

- *They Say/I Say* by Gerald Graff and Cathy Birkenstein is an invaluable, concise student textbook that offers templates for academic arguments.

- *Style: Ten Lessons in Clarity and Grace* by Joseph Williams offers wonderful ideas for writing better sentences and paragraphs, including exercises for students built right into the text.

- *Artful Sentences: Syntax as Style* by Virginia Tufte is a great professional development source for teachers interested in becoming more fluent in discussing verbs and other sentence parts.

- For a definition of an explication and more resources, Duke University provides a concise handout that may be used as a model of the kind of explication assignment one can create. See "Poetry Explication," http://uwp.duke.edu/uploads/assets/poetry.pdf.

- Purdue's Online Writing Lab (OWL) also has useful information regarding explication. See "Writing about Poetry," http://owl.english.purdue.edu/owl/resource/615/01/.

- *The Explicator* and the large body of work by Helen Vendler, Sven Birkerts, and other explicators and literary critics, such as Stephen Burt and Harold Bloom, are great sources for professional samples.

- "The Tone Map" lesson on the Poetry Out Loud website is wonderful for helping students develop a vocabulary for describing tone. See http://www.poetryoutloud.org/guide/The%20Tone%20Map%5B1%5D.pdf.

More on Curricular Debate

- The National Association for Urban Debate Leagues offers research and resources. See "Resources for Coaches and Debaters," http://www.urbandebate.org/coachanddebater_resources.shtml.

- Gerald Graff has written a number of books about the value of controversy in the classroom, including *Beyond the Culture Wars: How Teaching the Conflicts Can Revitalize American Education* and *Clueless in Academe: How Schooling Obscures the Life of the Mind.*

- Deanna Kuhn's research studies and her book *Education for Thinking* are wonderful professional development resources that explain why and how to use debate to engage students in critical literacy across disciplines.

- George Hillocks Jr. also provides valuable insight in his 2010 article "Teaching Argument for Critical Thinking and Writing: An Introduction."

Poems, Poets, and Poetry

Sir Thomas Wyatt, William Stafford, Walt Whitman, and Lorna Dee Cervantes are all widely anthologized, discussed, and published in a number of online sources.

Multimedia Resources

- "They Flee from Me" by Sir Thomas Wyatt (a recording of the poem), http://www.archive.org/details/audio_poetry_221_2007.

- "Beat! Beat! Drums!" by Walt Whitman (a choral and orchestral interpretation of the poem), http://www.youtube.com/watch?v=4MhnY_M_K9E&feature=related.

- "Drum-Taps (1865): A Machine Readable Transcription," *Walt Whitman Archive,* http://www.whitmanarchive.org/published/other/DrumTaps.html.

- "Freeway 280" by Lorna Dee Cervantes (a video recording of a reading of the poem), http://www.youtube.com/watch?v=AygCcaoMsZc.

Additional Scholarship for Authors Discussed in This Chapter

Blake, David Haven, and Michael Robertson. *Walt Whitman, Where the Future Becomes Present.* Iowa City: U of Iowa P, 2008. Print.

Estrin, Barbara L. *Laura: Uncovering Gender and Genre in Wyatt, Donne, and Marvell.* Durham: Duke UP, 1994. Print.

Foley, Stephen Merriam. *Sir Thomas Wyatt.* Boston: Twayne, 1990. Print.

Genoways, Ted. *Walt Whitman and the Civil War: America's Poet during the Lost Years of 1860–1862.* Berkeley: U of California P, 2009. Print.

Greenspan, Ezra. *The Cambridge Companion to Walt Whitman.* Cambridge: Cambridge UP, 1995. Print.

Kitchen, Judith. *Understanding William Stafford*. Columbia: U of South Carolina P, 1989. Print.

Mancuso, Luke. *The Strange Sad War Revolving: Walt Whitman, Reconstruction, and the Emergence of Black Citizenship, 1865–1876*. Columbia: Camden House, 1997. Print.

Miller, F. DeWolfe, ed. *Walt Whitman's* Drum-Taps *and* Sequel to Drum-Taps. Gainesville: Scholar's Facsimiles and Reprints, 1959. Print.

Morris, Roy, Jr. *The Better Angel: Walt Whitman in the Civil War*. Oxford: Oxford UP, 2000. Print.

Pinsker, Sanford. *Three Pacific Northwest Poets: William Stafford, Richard Hugo, and David Wagoner*. Boston: Twayne, 1987. Print.

Stafford, William, and William Heyen. *I Would Also Like to Mention Aluminum: Poems and a Conversation*. Pittsburgh: Slow Loris, 1976. Print.

Whitman, Walt. *The Sacrificial Years: A Chronicle of Walt Whitman's Experiences in the Civil War*. Ed. John Harmon McElroy. Boston: Godine, 1999. Print.

Assessment

■ Wormeli, Rick. *Fair Isn't Always Equal: Assessing and Grading in the Differentiated Classroom*. Portland: Stenhouse, 2006. Print.

Appendix: Student Handouts and Teaching Aids

Handouts		Chapter	Lesson
1.A	SOAPSTone	2	1
1.B	Key Literary Terms for Discussing Imagery	2	1
1.C	Think-Aloud Prompts	2	1
4.A	Getting Ready to Recite	2	4
5.A	Key Literary Terms for Discussing Poetic Forms and Techniques	3	5
5.B	More Think-Aloud Prompts	3	5
5.C	Getting Ready to Recite: "I Am Waiting"	3	5
5.D	Artful Writing: Composing Free Verse	3	5
5.E	Workshop Templates	3	5
6.A	Getting Ready to Recite: "'Hope' is the thing with feathers"	3	6
6.B	Artful Writing: Attending to Rhythm	3	6
7.A	Getting Ready to Recite: "If We Must Die"	3	7
7.B	Artful Writing: Exploring the English (Shakespearean) Sonnet	3	7
8.A	Artful Writing: Creating Sonic Patterns	3	8
9.A	Key Literary Terms for Discussing the Verb and Other Sentence Parts	4	9
9.B	Getting Ready to Recite: "They Flee from Me"	4	9
9.C	Developing Summaries of Poems	4	9
9.D	Describing Text Templates	4	9
9.E	Sample Explication: "They Flee from Me" (1557) by Sir Thomas Wyatt	4	9
9.F	Explication Rubric	4	9
9.G	Describing Text Think-Sheet	4	9
10.A	Sample Explication: "Traveling through the Dark" (1962) by William E. Stafford	4	10
10.B	Explication Workshop	4	10
11.A	Getting Ready to Recite: "Beat! Beat! Drums!"	4	11
11.B	Sample Explication: "Beat! Beat! Drums!" (1861) by Walt Whitman	4	11
11.C	Verbs for Describing Texts	4	11
12.A	Independent Study Reflection	4	12

Handout 1.A. SOAPSTone

Overview: When we begin reading a text, we should automatically start asking some questions to help us get the gist of a text before we begin analyzing it. Not every question posed here can be answered immediately, but exploring each one consciously throughout your reading process is essential.

S What is the subject of the piece? What is the general topic or idea of the piece?

O What is the occasion? What is the time, place, and setting of the piece? What is the situational context of the utterance?

A Who is/are the audiences? To whom is this utterance directed?

P What is the speaker's purpose?

S Who is the speaker?

Tone What is the tone of the piece as a whole? In other words, what tone of voice might this speaker use if he or she were to say this out loud? Remember that it changes throughout even the shortest poem, so consider plural answers to this question. Also ask what is the tone of each part of the text?

Handout 1.B. Key Literary Terms for Discussing Imagery

Detail: The features and elements an author chooses to include in a composition.
Example: In William Carlos Williams's "The Red Wheelbarrow," Williams includes only three details about the wheelbarrow; in addition to the color, he adds that it is "glazed with rainwater" and that it is "beside the white chickens." Those details place the red wheelbarrow in a distinct setting.

Diction: A poet's choice of words. In describing a writer's diction, one may refer to the use of a distinct dialect, colloquial versus formal word choices, abstract versus concrete, or specialized words from particular disciplines or discourse communities, among other aspects.
Example: In William Carlos Williams's "The Red Wheelbarrow," Williams borrows a word from the realm of visual art, "glazed," to describe the appearance of rainwater on the wheelbarrow. In borrowing this specialized term, which describes the process of creating a glassy appearance, he highlights his own role as an artist in the viewer's perception of the wheelbarrow.

Figurative Language: Language that implies ideas beyond the literal, often by suggesting comparisons between two things as in a simile or a metaphor.
Example: In *As You Like It,* when Shakespeare wrote, "All the world's a stage, / And all the men and women merely players; / They have their exits and their entrances," he used figurative language to suggest that humans, like actors, portray themselves differently, according to the various roles they assume throughout their lives.

Image: A word or phrase that appeals directly to the reader's senses (taste, touch, hearing, sight, or sound.)
Example: In his one-sentence poem "The Red Wheelbarrow," William Carlos Williams uses simple but vivid descriptions to help readers see the image of "a red wheelbarrow."

Metaphor: A type of figurative language in which one thing is said to be something else.
Example: In "Nothing Gold Can Stay," Robert Frost writes, "Nature's first green is gold / her hardest hue to hold." Frost suggests that new and pure things such as a new leaf are as rare and precious as the valuable metal gold.

Simile: A type of figurative language that makes a comparison between two unlike objects or ideas using the words *like* or *as*.
Example: In his poem "A Dream Deferred," Langston Hughes asks, "What happens to a dream deferred? / Does it dry up like a raisin in the sun?" The poet wonders if one possible result of putting off a dream is that it changes, becoming sweeter and more enduring, like raisins made from drying grapes in the sun.

Bonus Words: *Tenor* and *Vehicle*

Tenor: The original subject in a metaphor. Characteristics of the vehicle are applied to the tenor in a metaphor.

Vehicle: The object to which the original subject is compared and from which characteristics or attributes are borrowed.
Example: "My son (tenor) is a tornado (vehicle)." My son can create chaos and leaves a path of destruction in a moment of energetic play.

360 Degrees of Text: Using Poetry to Teach Close Reading and Powerful Writing by Eileen Murphy Buckley © 2011 NCTE.

Handout 1.C. Think-Aloud Prompts

This makes me picture . . .
(Imagery)

I imagine the speaker's voice sounding . . .
(Tone)

The speaker must be . . .
(Point of View)

The speaker is saying . . .
(Paraphrase)

The reason this speaker is saying this is because . . . and because . . .
(Character/Situation)

Based on the speaker's word choice, I am guessing . . .
(Diction)

I am puzzled because . . .
(Monitoring Comprehension)

I wonder why the author picked . . .
(Author's Craft)

This metaphor/simile makes me associate_____ with _____ because when most people think of _____, they think of _____.
(Analysis)

This metaphor/simile makes me wonder which qualities of _____ are associated with _____, because _____ is like _____, while _____ is/has _____.
(Analysis)

Handout 4.A. Getting Ready to Recite

Step 1: Choose a Poem and Use Your Close Reading Strategies
After selecting a text, perform a close reading. Visualize every image, think aloud about the author's choices, determine the antecedent scenario, and divide the poem into parts. Paraphrase the text until you are sure you have a lot to say about the rhetorical situation/SOAPSTone.

Step 2: Find the Emotional Build, Crisis, Climax, and Dénouement
A recitation gives body and voice to the emotional drama that unfolds in a poem. The speaker brings the audience on a journey of emotional peaks and valleys. A good performance, as opposed to a monotone calling out of memorized words, illustrates this variety in emotional intensity. The terms *build*, *crisis*, *climax*, and *dénouement* are helpful in thinking about how to find the emotional structure of a poem. (Explore the example provided on the next page to find out how these terms might apply to the poem "Facing It.")

When you are ready to think about how your performance should look and sound, start by zeroing in on the *build*, the expositional part of the text that gives the audience initial information about the SOAPSTone. This is the part of the poem that introduces basic facts and allows the audience to get a grip on the speaking situation. Who is speaking and why? To whom? How does the speaker sound? What is his or her tone? What kinds of gestures might he or she make?

Next find the *crisis*, a turning point or new idea, which points the audience toward the *climax*, the most intense moment of the poem. Ask yourself how might the tone of the speaker's voice change here? Does the volume or pitch change? Does the speaker's physical presence change?

Find the *climax* and consider how the rest of the poem should sound in comparison to the level of intensity in that climactic moment. Is it a whisper or a scream? Does it require a slow or fast-paced delivery? What gestures are fitting here?

Lastly, find the *dénouement*, or gradual decrease in intensity. It unravels the emotional climax and gives us closure. It doesn't necessarily exist in every poem, but when it does, it often illustrates a speaker's new understanding or emotional state. Think about how these last, powerful words will trickle off your tongue, leaving the audience in awe!
Adapted from Todd V. Lewis, *Communicating Literature*, 71

Step 3: Memorize and Rehearse
Memorization is easier than you think and essential to your performance. Memorize a chunk at a time, rehearsing enough to feel comfortable but not mechanical. Just try to own the words of the text enough to take the emotional journey of the speaker anew each time, without having to worry about your next line.

continued on next page

Build, Crisis, Climax, and Dénouement in "Facing It"

Example: *The Build*
My black face fades,
hiding inside the black granite.
I said I wouldn't,
dammit: No tears.
I'm stone. I'm flesh.
My clouded reflection eyes me
like a bird of prey, the profile of night
slanted against morning. I turn
this way—the stone lets me go.
I turn that way—I'm inside
the Vietnam Veterans Memorial
again, depending on the light
to make a difference.

The speaker begins the poem by telling us how he feels and where he is, involving the audience in his initial encounter with the physical space. This *build* walks the audience through each visual image and its emotional impact. As he moves from an examination of his own reflection (my black face) to the place (Vietnam Veterans Memorial), the speaker is building up the intensity of the drama, preparing the audience for understanding the enormity of the emotional crisis the speaker is about to face. While the most intense moment (*climax*) is yet to come, the build includes some emotionally intense moments—the moment where he is holding back tears, for example. In a recitation, some vocal and gestural indication of that intensity is called for here.

Example: *The Crisis*
I go down the 58,022 names,
half-expecting to find
my own in letters like smoke.
I touch the name Andrew Johnson;

The *crisis,* or turning point, comes at the moment the speaker touches the wall. It is the only tactile image in the poem. This is where the performer needs to end up by the end of the build, so the intensity of the climax (the flashback to a booby trap) doesn't seem melodramatic.

Example: The *Climax*
I see the booby trap's white flash,
Names shimmer on a woman's blouse
but when she walks away
the names stay on the wall.
Brushstrokes flash, a red bird's
wings cutting across my stare.

continued on next page

The sky. A plane in the sky.
A white vet's image floats
closer to me, then his pale eyes
look through mine. I'm a window.
He's lost his right arm

In the *climax,* the speaker brings the audience through the emotional wreckage of this moment of flashback, juxtaposing shard-like images that suggest the veteran's struggle to reconcile the absence of war with the living memory of war. This is a tall order for a performer. A steady *build* and a strong indication of the *crisis* will allow a good performer to pull off the emotionally explosive delivery of this moment of *climax.*

Example: *The Dénouement*
inside the stone. In the black mirror
a woman's trying to erase names:
No, she's brushing a boy's hair.

In the *dénouement*, the speaker brings the audience back to the memorial. At this point, the speaker is almost talking himself down from the peak, back into the world of now. It is powerful in that the speaker almost seems to leave off thinking about the pain of this experience, distracting himself with something else. Yet this image also suggests both a recognition that his personal experience is also a universal one, and that the painful memory and eternal threat of war also looms over the woman and the boy.

See one student's performance of "Facing It" at www.poetryoutloud.org.

360 Degrees of Text: Using Poetry to Teach Close Reading and Powerful Writing by Eileen Murphy Buckley © 2011 NCTE.

Handout 5.A.
Key Literary Terms for Discussing Poetic Forms and Techniques

Alliteration: The repetition of initial stressed, consonant sounds in a series of words within a phrase or verse line.
Example: In Jane Kenyon's poem "Let Evening Come" (1990), the *l* sound in the line "Let the light of the late afternoon" forms a pattern of alliteration.

Allusion: Written or spoken text intended to make an audience recall another thing, usually a well-known person or text. Allusions often refer to historical texts, as well as the Bible, and other literary and religious texts such as Greek and Roman myth.
Example: In Robert Frost's "Nature's Green Is Gold," the line "So Eden sank to grief" refers to the biblical story of Adam and Eve, who sinned in Eden and were forced to live with the consequence of facing their own mortality as a result of eating from the tree of knowledge of good and evil.

Assonance: The repetition of similar vowel sounds within a line or succeeding lines of verse.
Example: In "We Real Cool" (1959) by Gwendolyn Brooks: "Sing sin. We / Thin gin. We."

Consonance: Repetition of the same or similar consonant sounds in a line or succeeding lines of verse.
Example: In "Blackberry Picking" (1998) by Seamus Heaney: "we trekked and picked until the cans were full, / until the tinkling bottom had been covered."

Couplet: A pair of successive rhyming lines, usually of the same length.
Example: "The Rape of the Lock" (1714) by Alexander Pope: "What dire offence from am'rous causes springs, / What mighty contests rise from trivial things."

End-Stopped Line: When a line of verse ends at the end of a verse, sentence, or another complete grammatical unit such as an independent clause.
Example: From the opening lines of the poem "Battlefield" by Mark Turcotte:
"Back when I used to be Indian (Line break)
I am standing outside the (Enjambment)
pool hall with my sister." (End-stopped line)

Enjambment: When a line of verse ends before the end of the sentence or verse of which it is a part. (See the example following "End-stopped Line," a closely related term.)

Formal Meter: A regular pattern of stressed and unstressed syllables in a line of verse.
Example: In "'Hope' Is the Thing with Feathers" (1849) by Emily Dickinson: "And sings the tune without the words— / And never stops—at all—" is an example of an alternating unstressed syllable then stressed syllable pattern, which is a type of metrical foot called an iamb. Formal meter is usually described in terms that indicate the type of foot and the number of feet per line, as in iambic pentameter, which is five feet of iambs.

continued on next page

Free verse: Free verse is simply poetry that does not adhere to a particular metrical pattern and often follows the natural rhythms of everyday speech.
Example: See "I Am Waiting" (1958) by Lawrence Ferlinghetti.

Hymn: A poem praising God or the divine, which is often sung and traditionally follows an alternating rhymed eight-syllable, then six-syllable pattern.
Example: See "'Hope' is the thing with feathers" (1849) by Emily Dickinson.

Line Break: A line break in poetry refers to the end of line. (See the example following "End-Stopped Line," a closely related term.)

Quatrain: A verse stanza of four lines.
Example: From "Sonnet 130" by William Shakespeare:
    My mistress' eyes are nothing like the sun;
    Coral is far more red than her lips' red;
    If snow be white, why then her breasts are dun;
    If hairs be wires, black wires grow on her head

Sonic Patterns: The artistic arrangement and repeated, patterned use of sounds.
Example: From "Those Winter Sundays" by Robert Hayden:
    And put his clothes on in the blueblack cold,
    then with cracked hands that ached
    from labor in the weekday weather made
    banked fires blaze. No one ever thanked him

    The *b*, *k*, and *d* sounds are woven throughout these lines.

Sonnet: A fourteen-lined poem.
Example: See "If We Must Die" (1919) by Claude McKay

Stanza: An arrangement of a certain number of lines, usually four or more, sometimes having a fixed length, meter, or rhyme scheme, forming a division of a poem.
Example: See "This Is Just to Say" by William Carlos Williams for a brief example.

360 Degrees of Text: Using Poetry to Teach Close Reading and Powerful Writing by Eileen Murphy Buckley
© 2011 NCTE.

Handout 5.B. More Think-Aloud Prompts

I wonder why the author uses repetition here when he or she chooses . . .
(Patterns and Variations in Author's Craft)

There is a rhyming pattern here that goes . . .
(Patterns and Variations in Author's Craft)

I am starting to see a pattern of (sounds, images, topics, etc.) . . .
(Patterns and Variations in Author's Craft)

The poet seems to break a pattern of . . . when . . .
(Patterns and Variations in Author's Craft)

According to a strict definition, in the traditional form, this kind of poem has . . . ,
and/or/but this poem . . .
(Genre Awareness)

This seems like an allusion, because it makes me think of . . .
(Text-to-Text Connections)

If the end of this line were the end of the sentence, the line would mean . . .
(Author's Craft/Enjambment)

Handout 5.C. Getting Ready to Recite: "I Am Waiting"

Step 1: Use Your Close Reading Strategies

Visualize each image and research new words and phrases you suspect to be allusions to other texts. (Hint: Look for capitalized words.) Think aloud about the author's choices, paying special attention to line break, repetition, and allusion. Determine the antecedent scenario, divide the poem into parts, and paraphrase the whole text until you can identify the SOAPSTone. If you plan to use only part of the script, focus on a whole part, a whole stanza, and use the entire poem as a guide to the meaning of your section.

Step 2: Find the Emotional Build, Crisis, Climax, and Dénouement

Each stanza in this long poem has its own emotional beginning, middle, and end. Find the emotional curve of the text by looking for the following components. Don't worry if you can't find these parts in your selection. They aren't always immediately apparent and the build and dénouement are sometimes imperceptible or non-existent. The most important piece is the climax. Consider where your selection becomes most intense. Think about how the rest of the poem falls in relation to that intensity.

Build—Background information about this character and the situation.
Crisis—Turning point or change of idea that sets us up for the climax.
Climax—The most intense moment of the poem.
Dénouement—The unraveling that leads us back down from the peak and gives us closure.

Consider the ways in which key words and phrases might be played up with gesture and voice modulation (tone, pitch, volume, duration). Pay special attention to line breaks. This performance relies upon the humor of incongruities, the reversal of our expectations. The speaker often delivers surprising twists on conventional ideas using line break. The serious delivery of these comical lines is essential to hitting the punch line. When enjambment offers the opportunity for humor, try playing it up by experimenting with a few different approaches. Use a small section to see how these different plays would sound, but always use the larger sense of the poem as your guide.

- How would it sound if the speaker kept the same serious, zealous tone throughout the entire piece?
- How would it sound if the speaker was played as a smart, cynical guy, like a standup comic?
- How would it sound if you played the speaker as someone searching for the right word, stumbling into the humor of the piece after each line break?

Step 3: Memorize and Rehearse

Remember, this is a script. Know your lines and embody the character. Give yourself plenty of time for repeated rehearsals, and the memorization will come.

360 Degrees of Text: Using Poetry to Teach Close Reading and Powerful Writing by Eileen Murphy Buckley © 2011 NCTE.

Handout 5.D. Artful Writing: Composing Free Verse

Image Generator: Wish List

Free verse is a form. Though they do not always rely upon traditional metrics and rhyme patterns, free verse poets are every bit as concerned with rhythm, line breaks, sound devices, and other poetic tools as were the sonneteers and other formalists who preceded them. This is an opportunity for you to experiment with one of the most powerful tools of the free verse poet—line break.

List poems are great for generating images quickly. They also relieve you of the anxiety of writing a poem, instead offering you an invitation to create imagery. Using the first line of Ferlinghetti's poem "I Am Waiting" as a springboard—or not—write a wish list. Think, what would make your life better, more fun, more fulfilling? Think small, think big, think concrete, think abstract. You can stop at just one item as long as you provide plenty of vivid details about it, or you can go on and on, creating long lists.

Once you have a wish list or a vivid description of one or more items, arrange the list strategically. How do your images fit together? Is there an organic order to your list or does it need rearrangement? How can these images be grouped or divided?

Perhaps you wished for the ideal school. You might have started with physical characteristics, then location, amenities, the people you'd share it with, and so on. Play with different arrangements. Keep playing until you have found the best order for these images (for example, large to small, concrete to abstract, or first to last) until you find the one that works best.

Revision Strategy: Playing with Line Breaks

Try taking your list now and breaking the lines in new places. Find what you would consider the most important word in each line. Now break the line so that that word becomes the last word of the line. This final word in a line of poetry often takes on greater prominence than words in the middle of a line.

Another way to examine your line breaks is to ask, "Does the line break open up multiple interpretations of a single line?" In other words, if the sentence were to end where the line ended, would it mean something different? Investigate your poem, using these questions. If all else fails, you might try breaking the lines after the nouns. Then try breaking them after verbs or before prepositions. Does this affect the meaning of your line? Is the last word in each line deserving of such prominence?

Save and date your drafts, as you never know when you will discover that the first or the third draft best captured the sense you were striving toward.

Sharing Out Loud

Pair up with a partner and share your wish list. Give your partner a chance to prepare a reading, so they are able to take in all of the line breaks and other arrangements in the text. When your partner reads it aloud, make notes. Did it sound the way you wanted it to sound? Now read it aloud yourself. Did you find yourself stumbling? Mark those passages then use the Workshop Template (handout 5.E) to describe to each other the effect of images and other details, such as allusions, in terms of the overall goals of each composition. Be sure to use Key Literary Terms for Discussing Imagery (handout 1.B)

continued on next page

and Key Literary Terms for Discussing Poetic Forms and Techniques (handout 5.A) as you share feedback. It is important to honor your work and the work of your fellow writers with the same precise and sophisticated language you use in your close readings of published works.

"I Am Waiting" Student Sample

I am waiting for
the number on my bank statement
to get out of the red and
become infinitely green.
I am waiting for a library
to go on sale. A library
plus basement. A library
by day, a nightclub by night.
I am waiting for buckets of black paint
and a set of black lights
and a black shirt (or two)
and a few pairs of black tights.
I am waiting to
furnish my own nightclub.
Waiting, for time to disappear
into a big pink vortex
with 90's pop hits and winter holiday songs,
leaving happiness behind.
Reading to pass the happiness.
I wouldn't wait
to check out contemporary
and classic literature from my library.
I wouldn't wait
for friends to come around
waiting with or without their bad
romances to spend my happiness in my club
the flashing lights like stars on my black ceiling.
I'm a star.
And stars never wait
to just dance, dance.

Elizabeth, grade 11

360 Degrees of Text: Using Poetry to Teach Close Reading and Powerful Writing by Eileen Murphy Buckley
© 2011 NCTE.

Handout 5.E. Workshop Templates

Directions: Help the writer understand the effect of his or her current choices by describing the text. Write at least two complete sentences directly on the writer's work in the form of the Description Template.

Description Template

When____1__ said _____3_____, it made me think __4a___, because when most people think of __4b__, they think of __4c___ because . . .

The **2** appears above "said" and **4a** above portions.

Key
1 Who is the **choice maker?** (The author? The speaker?)
2 What **verb** best describes what the speaker did? (Described, said, did, chose, etc.)
3 What **choice** are you discussing? (Quote, image, word, technique, etc.)
4a–c What **associated meanings** come to mind with this text? (What do you picture and why? Have you seen this word, image, technique before? Would other readers make this connection? This is where you are explaining your interpretation. Your elaboration may take more elaboration, and so on.)

Excerpt from a Sample Student Poem "Hold" by Mickal McLendon (Grade 12)
You held my hand through winter,
Made tracks for me to follow,
And squeezed my hand when I fell behind—
A pulse that rippled to my toes,
Through cotton mitts
And my tiny bones.

Example Reviewer Claim Using Description Template:

When <u>the speaker</u> *described* <u>the person holding his hand in winter</u> **it made me think of a**
(1, 2 above "the speaker described", 3 below)

<u>parent showing a kid how to get through something</u> **because when most people think of**
(4a, 4b, 4c)

someone <u>holding a "tiny" hand,</u> **they think of** <u>a parent</u> **because** <u>a parent would make</u>

<u>tracks for a child to follow and hold their hand to help show them how to get through the</u>
(4a, 4b, 4c)

<u>snow</u> **and when most people think of** <u>the snow</u> **they think of** hard times **because** <u>it is</u>

<u>harder to get around in the winter.</u>

continued on next page

Directions: As you make suggestions, write in complete sentences directly on the writer's work when possible. Write at least two more sentences in the form of the Suggestion Templates. Make sure you reference specific places in the text, so the writer, who may not have time to digest all the suggestions in one sitting, can refer to them later. Also, if more than one reader makes suggestions about a particular area, the writer may see a pattern that will help guide their revisions. As always, be kind, encouraging, and precise!

Suggestion Template

You might consider (revising, describing, cutting) (word, image, section, technique, etc.)

because (I don't quite understand/I am unclear/I get confused) when . . .

Or, simply

In (line/sentence/section,) I would like to know more about . . .

Example

You might consider <u>using more concrete descriptions of the adult's physical appearance</u> to convey <u>how the child sees him,</u> so readers can better understand <u>how the speaker feels about him</u>. For example, I would like to know more about <u>how the expression on his face actually looks when he squeezed his hand.</u>

360 Degrees of Text: Using Poetry to Teach Close Reading and Powerful Writing by Eileen Murphy Buckley © 2011 NCTE.

Handout 6.A. Getting Ready to Recite: "'Hope' is the thing with feathers"

How does one handle a line break or a steady rhythm in reciting a metered poem? This question is fundamental to performing any verse, from Shakespeare to Dickinson to a contemporary poet like Kevin Young. The answer is that the performer is charged only with conveying the meaning of lines and sentences, not indicating how a scholar would scan the poem or how the text looks on a page.

Step 1: Not How the Poem Is Written but What the Speaker Says

Patsy Rodenberg, author of *Speaking Shakespeare*, likens an actor's work with meter to a pianist's work with a metronome. We don't see it during performance, but the rhythm awareness developed during practice stays with the pianist and "holds the performance together" (86). During a recitation, the performer should concentrate on what the speaker is saying, rather than how the poem is written, imagining the scenario and saying what needs to be said given the SOAPSTone.

Step 2: Identify the Build, Crisis, Climax, and Dénouement

Now bring your knowledge of the poem to bear on your character and consider this question: Why does the speaker need to define hope? To whom is this definition uttered? Why? In other words, what is the antecedent scenario that caused the speaker to speak at this moment? Commit to an interpretation and build your recitation around it, looking for ways to use your knowledge of key elements such as hymnal structures and rhythm along the way.

Build—Background information about this character and the situation.
Crisis—Turning point or change of idea that sets us up for the climax.
Climax—The most intense moment of the poem.
Dénouement—The unraveling that leads us back down from the peak and gives us closure.

Step 3: Consider Volume, Pace, Gesture

As you prepare, consider how the tools of public speaking can enhance your recitation. Play with all sorts of possibilities. Sometimes saying something quietly can be more powerful than saying it loudly. Slowing down a line, phrase, or a single word can also pack a huge punch. Consider one key gesture that might make an otherwise creatively subtle performance stand out.

Step 4: Don't Chant

Don't over-memorize or over-rehearse this rhythmic poem, as you might run the risk of falling into a chant. Try to keep it fresh. Don't forget, it is a short but rich text with loads of opportunity for vocal texture.

Handout 6.B. Artful Writing: Attending to Rhythm

Image Generator: Definition Poem

Take a concept. Any concept will do—hope, beauty, fear—something without a concrete reference in the world. Now define it. You could leap off of Dickinson's first line to begin by simply filling in the blanks: "(Concept) is the thing with (Noun)." As in Dickinson's poem, that first noun image may guide your choice of other images. Alternatively, you can simply generate images for your poem by telling us how this concept feels, tastes, smells, sounds, and looks using all five senses (another list poem). Capture your images in as many action verbs as possible.

When you have finished generating your list of images, think about how different arrangements of that list might work. Are the "best words in the best order"? What would happen if you attempted to create more unity in your images, focusing on images of nature, city life, or high school, rather than using images from each of these domains? What would happen if you mixed things up a bit?

If learning about rhythm is not your fancy, you may stop here. Creating a vivid image of the concept you have chosen to illustrate is as much as any poet can ask. However, if you want to experiment with rhythm, take a look at a basic revision strategy below.

Revision Strategy: Revising with Rhythm—The Adventure Option

If you'd like to toy with the rhythm of your poem, here's how you might start. Begin playing with line breaks. See if you can follow the hymn structure. Start with a line of eight syllables, then a line of six syllables, then eight again and six more, and so on, or choose a uniform number of syllables per line throughout the poem.

When you begin playing with line breaks, you will probably find yourself making changes to word choice and word order that may even lead to new metaphors or other devices. While I encourage you to have fun, I must also advise you that like any other formal element, achieving a certain syllable count should never take precedence over the truth of your idea or the beauty of your language. It is but one consideration.

Remember that counting syllables is not the real key to rhythm. Playing with the pattern of stressed and unstressed syllables is where the work begins. Remember in Dickinson's poem that first line did not have the prescribed eight syllables yet the poem in general fit the pattern. Take a look at where the stresses fall (three or four pairs of iambs—unstressed, stressed—per line is what you are aiming for). To begin, ask which syllables are stressed? Which are unstressed? Consider them in pairs, rather than as a line. By this I mean that if you were to use some kind of electronic device to graph a line of iambic tetrameter, the peaks and valleys that would be generated might look very uneven, yet the value/peak pattern would be detectable. Take the first line of Dickinson's poem: "'Hope' is a thing with feathers." The words *hope, thing,* and part of *feathers* are stressed, but each one is stressed in a slightly different way. It takes longer to say *hope* and *thing* than it takes to say the stressed *fea* of *feathers,* but they are all equal in the sense that they act as the stressed syllable in the pair of syllables that make up the iamb. While your six or eight syllables may or may not fit into a strict pattern of alternating unstressed and stressed syllables, breaking lines into three or four pairs of syllables can help you learn to detect which syllable in the pair is stressed.

continued on next page

To illustrate my suggestion, I'll take a line I wrote: "Joy squeals like an infant." There are 6 syllables. Do I have three iambic feet? In other words does the rhythm sound like this: "joy SQUEALS like AN inFANT" No. It sounds more like "JOY SQUEALS like an INfant" If I liked the way that sounded, I'd leave it. If I was a stickler for meter, I might try. "Like INfant SQUEALS is JOY." The change has caused me to take an active verb, *squeals,* and change it to a verb of being, *is.* The syntax has also changed, with the subject now coming at the end of the line. The other knock-on effect is that the sentence now sounds a little archaic and highfalutin, but depending on the effect I was attempting to achieve, I might go with this revision.

The point is, if I hadn't asked myself about rhythm, I may never have stumbled upon this other possibility. And that is what these exercises are all about. You, the writer, have to decide what effect you want, but you should always undertake the discovery process in order to seize on the best of all possibilities. Try playing with at least one line.

The real point of this exercise is not to write a poem that adheres to some random rules about meter. It is to show you that meter is one of the tools with which a poet can work. Playing with rhythm can help you see the different ways in which the same line may be written. Take it or leave it. It is up to you.

As always, you may choose to return to your original choices, but it is always interesting to see where other choices might take you. Save and date earlier drafts!

Sharing Out Loud

Reading aloud will help you determine which choice is more effective in giving life to your concept. Pair up and have your partner read the poem. Using the Workshop Template (handout 5.E), each partner should consider the ways in which the arrangement of images relates to meaning. Do these sentences actually sound fitting, given the imagery and the concept? If this approach is too technical, do it the old-fashioned way—just consider whether or not it sounds good!

Student Sample: "Fear is a bodiless thing"
Fear is a bodiless thing
invisibly preying on the faint-hearted
catching unknowing persons in its
unrelenting grasp

Whispingly whispers
terrifying promises for the future in their ears
As a feeling shoots through their souls
millions of phobias being set free
These people await this wind's chill
for running is fruitless
The breezes of fear can't be escaped
only embraced and then
         released
              Luria, Grade 11

Handout 7.A. Getting Ready to Recite: "If We Must Die"

Step 1: Practice Breathing and Articulating
Say each word of the poem separately. Make sure that every sound of every word is clearly heard. Exaggerate each sound to make the language come alive. You'll also feel your diaphragm working to push the air out of your lungs as you say these words. Stand up as you work through the poem, breathing and balancing your weight so you are physically ready to communicate the epic drama that unfolds in this poem. You must take the stage as a great leader.

Step 2: Mark Up the Sound of the Text
Examine your graph of the lines of the poem and consider the rise and fall of each. Mark your script according to lines or parts of lines with greater or lesser intensity. Mark up the pace as well. Which lines are slow? Which are fast? What chunks go together? Which parts must be given the gravity of standing alone? Which are loud? Soft?

Step 3: Identify the Build, Crisis, Climax, and Dénouement
Now bring your knowledge of the poem to bear on your character, and as you put it all together consider this question: What is at stake in this act of persuasion? Call your audience to action, remembering the consequences of inaction.

> *Build*—Background information about the situation.
> *Crisis*—Turning point or change of idea that sets us up for the climax.
> *Climax*—The most intense moment of the poem.
> *Dénouement*—The unraveling that leads us back down from the peak and gives us closure.

Again, each of these four parts may not be present in every text, but every text has a climax. Find out where other parts of the poem fall in relation to that climax.

Step 4: Memorize and Rehearse
This poem is only fourteen lines long. After all this close reading, much of the text is probably already securely in your memory bank. Additionally, the mnemonic devices or rhyme and repetition may make this piece easier to memorize than others. Vocals and gestures won't get stale upon rehearsing if you keep your mind on the speaker's rhetorical purpose. Remember what is at stake for your imagined audience!

360 Degrees of Text: Using Poetry to Teach Close Reading and Powerful Writing by Eileen Murphy Buckley © 2011 NCTE.

Handout 7.B. Artful Writing: Exploring the English (Shakespearean) Sonnet

Image Generator: A Poem of Persuasion

While the Shakespearean sonnet is renowned for its vivid characters and romantic themes, it is also celebrated as an artful approach to argumentation. For this exercise, you will be asked to write a persuasive argument in fourteen lines. Forget about the elements of rhyme and rhythm for now and concentrate instead on developing vivid imagery in each of your appeals. Generating enough vivid material to select and arrange fourteen effective lines of imagery is enough to keep any poet busy for a long time.

Your subject may be serious, as is McKay's, or more light-hearted, as you please. The point of this exercise is to help you explore the parts of the sonnet. Begin by brainstorming things you want or things you want to do. To acquire something—whether it's permission to do something or go somewhere, or admission, say, to a college, for example—usually requires some persuading. Why not knock your audience's socks off with a sonnet of persuasion?

After you select the subject, select a very specific audience and consider what would appeal to that audience. Is it a parent, a friend, a romantic interest, a college admissions officer? Who? What images would appeal to that person?

As you begin drafting, focus first on inventing images without worrying about the length or quantity of lines. You will do better to remember the hogs, the dogs, the monster, and the grave of McKay's poem than to count lines. The images of indignity, ruthlessness, unnatural evil, and death are captured more fully and more powerfully in these vivid pictures than in the labels I have just used to describe them. Therefore, vivid imagery, not quantities of lines, should be your only concern as you generate the initial material for your argument. You will surely find that this is easier said than done, so take your time in the brainstorming process, creating plenty of material from which to choose as you refine your draft. You want leftovers, not shortages, when you revise.

After you have illustrated your ideas through vivid imagery, try arranging the material into fourteen lines of similar length, with the aim toward persuading your audience of a particular desire or belief. Experiment with different arrangements. As you arrange the materials, consider how ordering images in different sequences might change their overall effect.

Revision Strategy: Developing the Quatrains and the Couplet

McKay's poem provides a proposed response to a problem, reasons for responding in this way, and a final call to action. To revise your piece, consider the sections of this fourteen-line poetic form (three quatrains and a couplet). Is there a distinct difference in the imagery, language, or purpose between the first quatrain and the second? What is the rhetorical function of each part? In other words, what is the speaker attempting to accomplish in each? The questions below may provide additional ideas for revision.

- Somewhere in the first four lines, have you stated a desire or belief?
- In the second and third quatrains, have you provided reasons why your audience should yield to your desire or adopt your belief?

continued on next page

- The couplet in McKay's poem illustrates the way a sonnet's close often provides a potent combination of all that has come before it. It is not a summary, but a climax that is built upon the base of the quatrains. Are the last two lines of your piece powerful or memorable? How do they relate to what has come before? Consider the choices in previous lines (details, imagery, diction, metaphors, similes, etc.).

Sharing Out Loud

The sonnet in this exercise might be presented like a persuasive speech. Ask a partner to present it to you in that manner. Give your partner time to prepare. Then mark your text as you listen. Consider the speaker's audience. Do the images appeal to this audience? Does the speaker's choice of images contribute to his or her own credibility with this audience? Do the reasons for agreeing with the speaker seem compelling enough to move this audience to action? Is the ending memorable, powerful? Be sure to use Key Literary Terms for Discussing Imagery and Key Literary Terms for Discussing Poetic Forms and Techniques as you share feedback. It is important to honor your work and the work of your fellow writers with the same precise and sophisticated language you use in your close readings of published works.

Student Sample

Sonnet to a College Admissions Officer

Consider, please, your presentation of the school:
"READ ALL OF THE INSTRUCTIONS CAREFULLY
AS DIRECTED ON THIS SITE, AND FOLLOW THEM
TO THE LETTER [you could sound less cranky, here]
BEFORE CALLING OR . . ." or what? Annoying you?
You seem to say: At our school, there are laws
against troubling the admissions staff.
On the web and in the mail, to students,
your attitude prevails—your stern indifference.
You want no interview? Too hard to read
a supplemental essay? *What hindrance!*
Please, you have a lot of power here
Who cares if applicants are made to feel uneasy?
you could try to use it graciously.

May, Grade 12

360 Degrees of Text: Using Poetry to Teach Close Reading and Powerful Writing by Eileen Murphy Buckley
© 2011 NCTE.

Handout 8.A. Artful Writing: Creating Sonic Patterns

Image Generator: Composing a Memory Option

As in Hayden's fourteen-line poem, which uses the dominant image of a self-sacrificing father tending a fire and polishing his son's shoes, certain memories of a loved one are often shorthand for much of what we feel and think about the person. Select a person who helped you, protected you, taught you, comforted you, cheered you up, or with whom you have had an intense encounter or a deeply emotional relationship.

Take one memory of that person and recompose it now, as a work of art. The moment that you choose should be a close-up of a single event or an image you have seen over and over again, no more than one hour long. For example, if you want to write about the person who helped you learn to ride a bike, focus in on a specific memory, perhaps the first minutes after the training wheels came off, and write about it in as much sensory detail as possible.

Start by simply recording as many concrete details as you can remember. Try to use all five senses. You may use these sentence starters to gather sensory details that you will later shape and mold into a finished piece.

- I saw . . .
- I smelled . . .
- I tasted (or "could taste the ") . . .
- I heard . . .
- I felt (not emotions, but physical sensations) . . .

Remember, at this point, you are generating images through a process of recalling a memory unique to your experience. No one else can write this memory as it is uniquely yours. You may shape and alter these images later to suit your artistic goals. Write pages and pages if you like. Don't worry about form yet; just write!

Revision Strategy: Revising through Sonic Patterns

Step 1: Go back to the images you have generated and circle words, phrases, and images that capture this person's essence and this event most concisely and vividly.

Step 2: Take the images you have circled and arrange them and rearrange them. Pare down what you have written to a few essential images. Aim for fourteen lines or sentences at most. *Try to include at least one image with a sound.*

Step 3: Can you find or select a perfect word? Is there one word that might connect on multiple levels to the rest of the poem, a word that carries an important sound along with its meaning? Try to find that key word, that gem, and see where the process takes you. Perhaps the word can be the title.

Step 4: Read your piece aloud, exaggerating the sounds of your words. Consider the sounds that are repeated. Do any sounds seem to recur throughout the piece? Mark these patterns and variations as you go. Use a different highlighter or marking for each sound so you can physically see the patterns you have consciously and unconsciously begun to develop. Use your mouth, ears, and eyes to see what your words have already given you.

> *Alternate Step 4:* If you have no repetition, choose one or two images or phrases that you might consider hot spots in the poem—related parts to which you would like to draw attention. Is there any possibility for highlighting these phrases or images through sound? Could a change in word choice create a connection through consonant sounds or vowel sounds?

continued on next page

Caution: As you consider revisions that might enhance these patterns, you should also keep in mind that good writing isn't about engineering sound to reinforce meaning. This strategy for revision offers only one way to think about how the elements of a text can come together on multiple levels. As a writer, you have to make decisions about how to balance the beauty of the spontaneous phrase with artful revision, because all too often, too much of a good thing doesn't work. In the end, you have to remember the wisdom of the great poet William Carlos Williams: "If it ain't a pleasure, it ain't a poem!"

Sharing Out Loud—A Workshop Guide
Choose someone to read your poem aloud. Allow your reader time to prepare by reading and rereading a couple of times until they have a basic grasp of the piece and can read with some fluidity. Partners should then use the workshop template to describe the person or relationship depicted in the poem and the effect of your choices so far. Ask follow-up questions to help your reader/performer be specific about his or her feedback. Asking the reader, "What made you think that?" will reveal much of what your text tells the audience.

Sample Student Poem "Hold" by Mickal McLendan (Grade 12)
You held my hand through winter,
Made tracks for me to follow,
And squeezed my hand when I fell behind—
A pulse that rippled to my toes,
Through cotton mitts
And my tiny bones.
The wet flakes on my face
Were like a porcelain skin;
And I kept my head down lest I fall and break
As so many of my frozen tears.
(Hold onto me now.)
You cradled me against your shoulder,
And let me wrap my arms around your neck.
Looking up then to your locked jaw,
I thought, just once,
I'd see you shiver.
No. Not I.
Looking past you then
To see that pale and hollow tree
That had seen too many winters.
How warm it must be,
To crawl and curl inside
Where the world cannot
Harm its fragile things.
I thought to ask you . . .
You set me down.
You and I were past the crossing;
And once again you held my hand,
And I, I followed in your tracks.

360 Degrees of Text: Using Poetry to Teach Close Reading and Powerful Writing by Eileen Murphy Buckley © 2011 NCTE.

Handout 9.A. Key Literary Terms for Discussing the Verb and Other Sentence Parts

Active Voice: The agent of action is named.
Example: "I broke the vase." The subject of the sentence, "I," performed the action of breaking the vase.

Adjectival Phrase: A group of words in a sentence that performs the function of describing a noun.
Example: "A funny girl, Miriam was used to getting a lot of laughs." In this sentence, "a funny girl" is the adjectival phrase describing Miriam. Within the phrase, the article "a" and adjective "funny" both describe "girl."

Adverbial Phrase: A group of related words that together modify a verb, adjective, or other adverb. Adverbs indicate time, place, frequency, intensity, and manner (the manner in which something was done, such as "quickly").
Example: "Chris and I have to finish this project before winter break." In this sentence the adverbial phrase is "before winter break." It behaves in the sentence like an adverb of time. A good test for identifying an adverbial phrase is to try replacing it with a single adverb of time. In this case, "beforehand" could replace the whole phrase.

Agent: The person or animated thing that performs the action of the verb.
Example: "The car stopped." The agent who performed the action is "the car."

Complex Sentence: A sentence containing an independent clause and one or more dependent clauses.
Example: "After I came home, I took a shower." This complex sentence is made up of an independent clause, "I took a shower," and a dependent clause, "after I came home." Even though "I came home" is an independent clause, once the word "after" is added, it becomes dependent on the other part of the sentence to be a complete thought, because "after I came home" cannot stand alone.

Compound Sentence: A sentence containing two independent clauses.
Example: "You can make a salad at home, or you can go out for a pizza." This compound sentence is made up of two independent clauses that could stand alone: (1) "you can make a salad at home" (2) "you can go out for a pizza." In this case, the two clauses are joined by the conjunction "or." A semicolon might have been used to join these two sentences rather than the comma and conjunction.

Compound-Complex Sentence: A sentence with at least two independent clauses and one or more dependent clauses, joined by conjunctions and relative pronouns.
Example: "Kathy went to the store, but she couldn't buy groceries, because she forgot her wallet." This compound-complex sentence is made up of two independent clauses that could stand alone as their own sentences: "Kathy went to the store"

continued on next page

and "she couldn't buy groceries" as well as one dependent clause, "because she forgot her wallet," which is not a stand-alone, complete thought.

Passive Voice: The agent of the verb is not named.
   Example: "The vase was broken." The subject of the sentence, "the vase," is acted upon by something else. Even when a prepositional phrase is added, the sentence is still written in the passive voice because the subject undergoes action but does not perform the action of the verb. For example, "The vase was broken by me" is written in the passive voice, even though we know who did the action.

Predicate: The part of a sentence that expresses the action or the state of being.
   Example: "The fur interior was red." "The luxurious car rolled to a stop." While the predicating verb in the first sentence is "was," the complete predicate is "was red." The predicating verb in the second sentence is "rolled," and the complete predicate is "rolled to a stop."

Simple Sentence: An independent clause containing a subject and a verb expressing a complete thought.
   Example: "Judy walked her dog." This simple sentence contains a subject, "Judy," a verb, "walked," and expresses one complete thought.

Speech Act: The use of words to perform an action.
   Example: Saying "Forgive me" is an action. It acknowledges a wrongdoing or error and asks the question, "Will you pardon my wrongdoing?"

Subject: Who or what the sentence is about or the performer of the main action (predicating verb) in a sentence.
   Example: "The car had red fur interior." "The luxurious car rolled to a stop." In both sentences, the "car" is the subject.

Syntax: The meaningful relationships between parts of a sentence and sentence structure.
   Example: "A boy smiled at a girl" or "A girl smiled at a boy." Though the words are the same in both sentences, because of the order of the words, the meaning of the sentence changes.

Verb: A class of words that denotes an action or state of being or the relationship between things.
   Example: "The car stopped." The action word or verb is "stopped."

360 Degrees of Text: Using Poetry to Teach Close Reading and Powerful Writing by Eileen Murphy Buckley © 2011 NCTE.

Handout 9.B. Getting Ready to Recite: "They Flee from Me"

Whether this poem is performed as the lamentations of a jilted lover speaking to his bosom buddy or as an interior monologue, there are many familiar aspects of this character. This familiarity can cause a performer with a deep understanding of the character to swallow the speaker's words by assuming the mannerisms of the contemporary young cavalier of television sit-coms or, worse, fake a British accent. Just have fun, speak clearly, and capitalize on the potent language!

Step 1: Practice Breathing and Articulating

Say each word of the poem separately. Make sure that every sound of every word is clearly heard. This will be a workout for your lips, jaw, and tongue. You'll also feel your diaphragm working to push the air out of your lungs as you say these words. Stand up as you work through the poem, breathing and balancing your weight so your physical presence and the boom of your voice reflects the gigantic but fragile ego of your speaker.

Step 2: Play Up Agency

After you have worked through the poem a few times, zero in on the agent of action. You may even want to experiment with giving these actors and their actions a little more stress, the way you used to when you were telling on your little sister or brother. After all, this is a kind of he said/she said poem isn't it? (THEY flee from ME that sometime did ME seek). Practice saying a few lines in this way, playing up the agent and action.

Step 3: Identify the Build, Crisis, Climax, and Dénouement

Now bring your knowledge of the poem to bear on your character, and consider this question: How does he feel about what transpired between himself and the woman? Walk your audience through this man's experience as he relives these moments in his own mind. Think first and foremost about why he is telling his audience this story. Use the following framework to guide you through a plan for using your voice and gestures to successfully convey the emotional drama of the poem.

Build—Background information about this character and the situation.
Crisis—Turning point or change of idea that sets us up for the climax.
Climax—The most intense moment of the poem.
Dénouement—The unraveling that leads us back down from the peak and gives us closure.

Handout 9.C. Developing Summaries of Poems

The Definition

Components of a strong summary of a poem

- Brief explanation of the topic, action, or subject of the poem, indicating your take on the possible antecedent scenario and key aspects of the rhetorical situation or SOAPSTone.
- The name of the poem.
- The complete name of the author. You can shorten it to just the LAST name later in your discussion. Never call the author by his or her first name.
- A summary of a brief poem is often limited to a sentence or two.

Example:
In Sir Thomas Wyatt's "They Flee from Me," the speaker recounts his romantic exploits, focusing on one woman in particular who had a deep impact on him.

A summary may be more or less elaborate than this one, but this example represents the basic components that ought to be present.

Your Task
Write a brief summary of the poem. Use the SOAPSTone below to think through your summary before composing a sentence or two.

Author

Title

Speaker?

Occasion?

Audience?

Purpose?

Subject?

Tone

After thinking through pertinent details, compose a summary of your chosen poem and record it on a separate sheet of paper.

360 Degrees of Text: Using Poetry to Teach Close Reading and Powerful Writing by Eileen Murphy Buckley © 2011 NCTE.

Handout 9.D. Describing Text Templates

Scholars across academic disciplines interpret from the point of view that texts are products of a maker's choices. Whether they are analyzing fashion, poetry, political speeches, or visual and performing arts, the task of an interpreter/explicator is to make claims about the intended and unintended effects of the maker's choices. Please note, while the templates below can act as a formula of sorts for developing larger or smaller claims about text, they are not necessarily intended to represent sentences. Each component simply represents a *part* typically included in an interpretive claim or subclaim, regardless of how many sentences it takes to express the claim.

Sample Large Claim: (William Carlos Williams's poem "The Red Wheelbarrow") William Carlos Williams describes a farm scene using unusual line breaks and simple, yet suggestive diction to help the reader explore the role of art and artists in our perceptions of reality.

Large Claim Template

William Carlos Williams   describes
Choice Maker   *Verb for Describing Text*

a farm scene using unusual line breaks and simple, yet suggestive diction
Choice
(idea, image, technique, etc.)

to help the reader explore   the role of art and artists in our perceptions of reality.
Verb for Describing Text   *Interpreted Meaning*

This writer claims to know what the poem is about, but now she has a lot of explaining to do. Note that the adjectives "unusual" and "simple, yet unexpected" interpret as they describe. The phrase "to help the reader explore" implies the interpreter's judgments about images, line breaks, diction, and the author's intention. These implications also require further explanation. Additional *subclaims* will be needed to help readers understand some of these unspoken associated meanings.

Subclaim Template
Subclaims make up the majority of most interpretive writing. Subclaims involve elaborations on the effect of particular choices. Multiple subclaims might be needed to explain *how* and *why* a certain aspect of the text means what the interpreter claims it

continued on next page

means. Subclaims help interpreters to spell out, step by step, the valid connections between the text and the interpreted meaning. Just as in the Writing Workshop Template, subclaims also involve explaining connections to knowledge from outside the text. The textual evidence is essential to claims. Without the evidence, claims cannot be validated. A variety of textual references can be found in great paragraphs. Direct quotes, paraphrase, and summary can be woven directly into subclaims or appear before, after, or within the subclaim statements themselves.

The (detail, diction, image, etc.) (has the effect of _____) because _____ can be like _____ because when most people think of _____, they think _____, because _____.

Sample Subclaim (Robert Frost's "The Road Not Taken")
The image of two roads suggests that the decisions we make in life are like forks in a road, because as we move from one place in our lives to another, there are often several possible directions to take.

The image of two roads   suggests
          Choice   *Verb for Describing Text*
(detail, diction, image, etc.)   (has the effect of____)

that the decisions we make in life are like forks in a road
                    Associated Meanings
                    (because ____can be like___)

because as we move from one place in our lives to another, there are often several possible directions to take.

                    Interpreted Meaning
                          (because when most people think of ___, they think . . .)

(Explains the connection between particulars of the text and more general association to personal experience, another text, or some other aspect of the world outside the text.)

360 Degrees of Text: Using Poetry to Teach Close Reading and Powerful Writing by Eileen Murphy Buckley
© 2011 NCTE.

Handout 9.E. Sample Explication: "They Flee from Me"(1557) by Sir Thomas Wyatt

In "They Flee from Me," readers learn about a speaker's romantic past as he recounts his exploits and one particular experience with a special woman who had a deep impact on him. The speaker seems as familiar to a reader of the twenty-first century as a character from a favorite sit-com. He is a macho man with a heart—often despicable yet somehow lovable. Maneuvering the agent of action masterfully, Sir Thomas Wyatt draws a vivid picture of the jilting of a comical egotist.

A close examination of agency reveals a number of interesting moves the poet uses to characterize the speaker of this poem. Using two verbs in the first line—"flee" and "seek"—Wyatt introduces the main actors of the poem: various women from the speaker's romantic life and himself, a man who isn't always desperate, as he's careful to note. However, the agent of the second line, when the line is taken as a separate unit of meaning rather than part of the sentence, is not as clear. Who is doing the stalking and who is the prey? In either role—the innocent victim of amorous women or a powerful hunter—the speaker seems to come out ahead.

Wyatt's narcissistic character takes on another distasteful dimension in the rest of the stanza, "I have seen them gentle, tame, and meek, / That now are wild and do not remember / That sometime they put themself in danger / To take bread at my hand; and now they range, / Busily seeking with a continual change." Every action the speaker has "seen" seems to have been performed not by a woman but by a deer or some other creature, betraying the speaker's chauvinism.

"Thanked be fortune it hath been otherwise," opens the next stanza, as the speaker continues his brag. After he disparages the women who have turned from him, he focuses on one lover "in special." To capture the anticipation of newfound love, the speaker delays the verb, only hinting at the true agent in the next three lines which is made up of a series of prepositional and adverbial phrases. Not surprisingly, given the nature of the subject, it is a "gown" who then performs an action by falling right in the middle of the poem. At this halfway point, though, there seems to be a transformation of sorts when the agent "she" is introduced. It is "she" who owns the actions "caught," "kiss", and "said." This special woman even speaks for herself in the provocative quote, "Dear heart, how like you this?" Returning to his deer imagery by using the homonym for hart—the name of a male deer—he suggests that this question was evidence of a woman's sweet revenge rather than a sexually provocative query. Either way, judging from his rhetorical generosity here, he seems to have met his match in this woman.

If the speaker has not yet won the heart of the reader, the last stanza may have the power to endear him. The braggart declares, "It was no dream: I lay broad waking." Then he continues more humbly, giving equal agency to the woman who has given him "leave to go of her goodness / and she also, to use newfangledness." Whether it is a bitter lament or a sigh of regret, the speaker's attitude toward women in the end is intriguing.

Whether or not he is willing to recognize equality, he has certainly conceded a certain amount of power to this one woman in particular. The tone of this last stanza, shaped by the poet's choices regarding agency, suggests some evolution in his attitude. "She" is not portrayed as the meek animal taking food from his hand as the man of the first stanza might have it, but as another human being, a woman who wields a fair amount of power over him.

360 Degrees of Text: Using Poetry to Teach Close Reading and Powerful Writing by Eileen Murphy Buckley © 2011 NCTE.

Handout 9.F. Explication Rubric

	Excellent	Good	Fair	Poor	Unacceptable
Development and Thematic Discussion	Articulates a theme of the poem that requires careful analysis and close reading to understand.	Articulates a major theme of the poem using both surface and deeper details.	Articulates a basic, surface-level idea of the poem.	Misinterprets the major themes of the poem.	Does not discuss the major themes of the poem.
Evidence	Uses several key elements of the poem to support analysis.	Uses several elements of the poem to support analysis.	Uses some elements of the poem to support analysis.	Only uses surface-level elements to support analysis.	Does not give evidence to support the analysis.
Presentation of Evidence	Uses a variety of techniques to present evidence, including paraphrase, summary, and quotation. The integration of evidence is fluid.	Uses a variety of techniques to present evidence, including paraphrase, summary, and quotation. The integration of the evidence is sometimes fluid but awkward or jarring in some places.	Only uses two techniques to present evidence. The integration of the evidence is sometimes fluid but awkward or jarring in some places.	Uses one or two techniques to present evidence. The integration of the evidence is awkward or jarring.	There is no evidence presented.
Grammar and Mechanics	This paper has been proofread. There are very few errors in grammar and mechanics.	This paper has been proofread. However, there are some errors in grammar and mechanics.	This paper has several errors in grammar and mechanics but is still completely understandable.	This paper has many errors in grammar and mechanics. It demonstrates poor control over academic English.	The paper has so many errors in grammar and mechanics that it lacks fluency.

Handout 9.G. Describing Text Think-Sheet

Large Claim Template
Sample: In "Still I Rise," Maya Angelou uses a series of historically significant images to illustrate the struggles and triumphs of Africans and African Americans.

Maya Angelou	uses	a series of . . . to illustrate	the struggles and . . .
Choice Maker	*verb*	*Choice* *verb*	*Interpreted Meaning*
		(idea/image/technique, etc.)	

What major idea or theme did you construct based on your close reading? For example, does the author make an observation on the nature of human beings or societies? Does the text pose an important question, such as "Can we retain our ethnic identity and still be American?" What general judgment can one make about situations like the one described in the poem "Hope persists even under the worst circumstances"?

Interpreted Meaning_____

What particular words, images, phrases, or techniques made you think about these ideas? In other words, what element or technique in the text will you focus on in your discussion of the poem?

Choice (s)_____

Explain why these choices validate the interpreted meaning you inferred. Think back to your workshop template. "When the author said X, it made me think Y, because when most people think of X, they think of . . ." Explain, explain, explain.

Associated meanings

_____

_____

_____

Though we attribute every choice in the making of a poem to the poet, sometimes in our discussion of the poem, it makes more sense to say "the speaker, or the female character" since we don't know for sure if the speaker is the poet or a persona created by the poet. As you construct your overall claim about the poem, you have to decide who is responsible for the action(s) you are describing: the speaker, another character, or the poet. Who is the choice maker in your main claim?

_____

continued on next page

Your Turn to Construct a Claim

Now, on a separate sheet of paper, use the Describing Text Templates to write an opening paragraph with a summary and claim that you will support throughout your explication!

Your author	the technique(s) you will discuss	Major idea or theme you constructed
Choice Maker	verb *Choice* verb (*idea, image, technique, etc.*)	*Interpreted Meaning*

Student Samples

Sir Thomas Wyatt's "They Flee from Me" tells the story of a man and one woman who had a significant impact on him. Through his use of adjectives, the author allows the reader to wonder why humans react the way they do in romantic relationships.

William, Grade 12

Through diction and imagery, William Stafford expressed that in life there is a destination, but just like traveling in the dark, you will never know the obstacles in your path.

Gunnar, Grade 11

In her poem "Freeway 280" Lorna Dee Cervantes paints a portrait of the demise of a Spanish culture, buried within a cold and unnuturing city sprawl. She creates this dismal scene through the incorporation of dark and morbid imagery, Spanish language and phrase, and a personified culture and cityscape set in opposition to one another.

Pat, Grade 12

In "Those Winter Sundays," the author uses imagery to convey deep emotions of remorse over the sacrifices made by his father.

Jasmine, Grade 11

More Sample Sentences from Professional Explications

These samples come from professionally authored explicative writing. The selections illustrate the Describing Text Templates that lay beneath many of the sentences found in writings about literature. Every sentence does not necessarily contain all the constituent parts, but many sentences can be described in terms of the *choice maker, choice, associated and interpreted meanings* template. Like explications of poems, scholarly essays about all manner of subjects are made up of these claim-making sentences.

Sample Summary (Whole Poem): "They Flee from Me"

Wyatt's lyric famously describes a male lover who feels abandoned by all the women who once flocked to his bed.

continued on next page

Comment: *Note that this summary also makes a claim of sorts. To say he "feels abandoned" is different than saying he feels "bitter" or "regretful." So sometimes even summarizing in literary analysis involves making interpretative claims.*

Sample Summary (Stanza): "They Flee from Me"
The speaker reminisces about one paramour [lover], in particular, who came into his room one night, bared one of her shoulders, took him into her arms, kissed him, and then asked him whether he had enjoyed the whole experience.

Comment: *This sample is the explicator's interpretive summary of the whole second stanza.*

Sample Sentence within a Paragraph: "They Flee from Me"
In a classic response to this encounter, Wyatt's startled speaker declares, "It was no dreame, for I lay broade awakyng."

Comment: *Frequently explicators weave text directly into interpretive sentence. This explicator describes a particular moment in the speaker's emotional drama (interpreted meaning), illustrating how the author's use of the declarative sentence (choice) reveals the speaker's startled tone. The opening of the sentence indicates associated meanings, because the author calls the speaker's response "a classic response," suggesting that this shock is the response that most people in his situation would have.*

Sample Sentence within a Paragraph: "They Flee from Me"
He obviously feels almost a need to convince himself that this seduction really happened.

Comment: *This sentence exemplifies the classic "interpreted meaning" statement. This stand-alone sentence, containing no text, explains why the poet chose to include a particular element (a declarative sentence) or use a particular technique in the creation of a character. Unlike the large claim sentence that indicates the larger theme or idea of the poem as a whole, this subclaim asserts a particular interpretation of a specific line.*

Source: *Dan R. Davies and Robert C. Evans, "Jonson Alludes to Wyatt's 'They Flee from Me,'" Notes and Queries 47.1 (2000): 104.*

Sample Summary Sentence: "Still I Rise"
The single strongest affirmation of life is the title poem, "And Still I Rise." In the face of "bitter, twisted lies," "hatefulness," and "history's shame," the poet promises not to surrender.

Comment: *This sentence is taken from a paragraph discussing Maya Angelou's collection of poems And Still I Rise. The summary of the poem "Still I Rise" includes an example of how text can be woven into the summary itself. Also note the way in which the summary of this poem asserts a specific claim about the identity of the speaker and the intention of the poet.*

Source: *R. B. Stepto, review of And Still I Rise, by Maya Angelou, Parnassus 8.1 (1979): 313–15; rpt. Poetry Criticism, vol. 32 (Detroit: Gale, 2001).*

continued on next page

Sample Claim Sentence: "Still I Rise"
But the "I" of Angelou's refrain is obviously female and, in this instance, a woman forthright about the sexual nuances of personal and global struggle.

Comment: *This sentence, which was used to introduce the third to last stanza of the poem ("Does my sexiness upset you?"), makes a claim about the speaker's persona (interpreted meaning.) The explicator argues that this persona is developed through the poem's images and the use of "I" (choice). The sentence suggests that the poet's choices have to do with "the sexual nuances of personal and global struggle" (associated meanings,) and indicate ideas about larger issues beyond the text. In this case, the interpreter assumes readers share a knowledge base that will allow them to interpret the text in the same way she does.*

Source: Carol E. Neubauer, "Maya Angelou: Self and a Song of Freedom in the Southern Tradition," *Southern Women Writers: The New Generation*, ed. Tonette Bond Inge (Tuscaloosa: U of Alabama P, 1990): 114–42; rpt. Infotrac Contemporary Lit Crit.

Sample *Critical* Claim Sentence: "I Go Back to May 1937"
This passage is pure Olds formula: the skinny but irregular column, the typical enjamb-ment between article and noun, the overwrought similes which never quite work ("red tiles glinting like bent / plates of blood behind his head"), the relentless parallelism ("they are," "they are"). There is something really disturbing about this passage—not in the way Olds intended—in how formulaic it is.

Comment: *Even the most respected poets and poems can and must be discussed critically. Part of the work of a scholar is to argue about the merit of works of art. Sometimes scholars make criti-cal claims like this one, often prompting another critic to defend the work. Such critical debates are at the core of scholarly work. Students, too, should not shy away from making critical claims but should strive to support such claims with good explicative writing!*

Source: Terri Brown-Davidson, "The Belabored Scene, the Subtlest Detail: How Craft Affects Heat in the Poetry of Sharon Olds and Sandra McPherson," *Hollins Critic* 29.1 (1992): 1–10; rpt. *Poetry Criticism,* vol. 22 (Detroit: Gale, 1998), p. 318.

Handout 10.A. Sample Explication:
"Traveling through the Dark" (1962) by William E. Stafford

In his poem "Traveling through the Dark," William Stafford explores the relationships between humans and nature. The speaker tells of his encounter with a doe by the side of a narrow canyon road, dead, yet still pregnant with a living fawn. He gets out of his car, stumbles back to where the deer has been killed, and after a moment of pause, finally heaves the animal into the canyon. Obliged to clear the road for others despite his feelings of shame, the moment prompts him to consider how human beings navigate the ethical complexities of living in the modern, yet still natural world. Along with his provocative use of imagery, the speaker's crisis is mirrored in the intricate manipulation of agency, syntax, and sentence type.

Stafford's use of imagery plays upon the tension between the general and particular, the tension at the core of any ethical dilemma. The first line's idyllic, unadorned imagery of a lone traveler encountering a deer while traveling through the dark abruptly ends after the first line-break with the thudding sound of the word "dead." This generic scene of a man encountering an animal in the wilderness comes into focus with particulars in the next two lines when readers learn the deer is dead, on the "edge of the Wilson River road." The specificity of the speaker's description lays the groundwork for the building tension that began when humans settled this deer's wilderness, making roadways for cars and putting names to rivers as they mapped new territories.

The juxtaposition of the generic and specific continues through the end of the first stanza. Using the infinitive form of verbs as subjects and the pronoun "them" the speaker avoids assigning particular agents or recipients of action when he describes the general rule applied to these situations: "It is usually best to roll them into the canyon." In the next line, "that road is narrow; to swerve might make more dead," again no agent is responsible for the action of making more dead, however, the definite pronoun "that" suggests the speaker's recognition of the role he must play, the moral imperative that compels him to exit the car and take action because of the specific circumstance.

The speaker's initial certainty begins to flag once he exits the vehicle and enters the natural world. In contrast to the opening image, there are no passive constructions; the speaker and the deer are clearly the agents of all the actions as he moves out of the purely practical human world into an intimate encounter with another creature. As he describes his next steps, the unusual syntax reflects this sudden instability. "By glow of the tail-light I stumbled back of the car." No longer acting with the confidence of a moral imperative, the syntax causes the reader to stumble a little. "I stumbled back of the car," as opposed to "stumbled [to] the back" or "[in] the back of [the] car." The colloquial, phrasal verb "stumbled back," along with "stood by," mirrors his sudden lack of certainty as he moves from car to deer in the unnaturally lighted path to the "heap."

The closer he gets, the more particularized the deer becomes: "a doe, a recent killing," the victim of an untimely death, caused by another passing vehicle. As he drags her "stiffened," "almost cold" body off the narrow road, he refers to her as "she" and notes that she is "large in the belly," not yet comprehending her pregnancy.

The middle stanza focuses solely on the impact of his physical contact with the doe's body. "My fingers touching her side brought me the reason—" The poet's dazzling selection of the agent, fingers, in this sentence illustrates how the tactile rather

continued on next page

than rational perception of the creature initiates a new connection to her, plunging the speaker into her world, far from the certainty of human practicality.

The rules governing dead deer on the side of the canyon roads come into question after this touch when he discovers "her side was warm; her fawn lay there waiting, / alive, still, never to be born." The dangerous heap, cold and stiff, in the first stanzas becomes at this moment a mother and her fawn, the victims of a tragic fate, and is added to his universe of obligation. Punctuating the stanza and stopping readers in our tracks, the speaker's empathy, sadness, and his temporary inaction is captured in the poem's only end-stopped line containing a complete simple sentence: "Beside that mountain road I hesitated."

Reflecting his imbalance as he attempts to reconcile his conflicting obligations, the speaker returns to more complicated syntax in the fourth stanza. Made up of two independent clauses, the opening images add the surprising twist of personifying the vehicle, making it the active agent who has recalled the speaker to the human world and seems to have both animal and human qualities. Because readers are unprepared for the personification, the beginning of the line, at first, reads like the speaker's adjectival description of the position of the car, "aimed ahead" as if the speaker's view is panning outward to the larger scene. But the complete clause, "The car aimed ahead its lowered parking lights;" actually suggests that the car, too, pauses, perhaps with respect as indicated by the "lowered parking lights," yet waits, as if to remind the speaker their journey must continue. Again in the second independent clause, the speaker's perception of the car's superior calm is revealed. In the line, "under the hood purred the steady engine," the speaker reverses typical subject-followed by-predicate syntax, a nuance that heightens our awareness of the car's cat-like contentment with its ethically neutral function to propel us forward.

Shamed by the entire situation, the speaker's anxiety is juxtaposed with the purring of the single-purposed car in the last lines of the stanza, "I stood in the glare of the warm exhaust turning red; / around our group I could hear the wilderness listen." By the end of the encounter, the car, the doe and her fawn, and the wilderness itself seem to highlight the precariousness of being human, the difficulty of being ethical.

In the final couplet, "I thought hard for us all—my only swerving—," the speaker ratifies his decision to yield to his obligations to human beings, fellow travelers. As shameful as the act of disposing of the deer's body with her living fawn may be, his addition of "—my only swerving—" suggests that he is certain that bequeathing these bodies to the river is the right thing to do. The speaker, "then pushed her over the edge into the river." Notably, the predicate "pushed" shares the subject "I" in the previous clause, the speaker has no pronoun in the last line, but the particular identity of the deer is honored with the pronoun "her."

The rightness of the decision is affirmed with the final image of the river. Like all natural bodies of water, it holds the power to cleanse and to renew life. Parallel to the canyon road, this river also acts as nature's roadway, propelling everything forward.

The design of these last lines brings closure to the intricacies of the complex idea he explores throughout the poem, illustrating the very nature of ethical dilemma, where general rules seem inappropriate in a particular situation. Ethical decision-making is, at its core, as hard for all of us as traveling through the dark on a narrow canyon road, yet it is exactly what makes us human.

360 Degrees of Text: Using Poetry to Teach Close Reading and Powerful Writing by Eileen Murphy Buckley © 2011 NCTE.

Handout 10.B. Explication Workshop

Read and mark the paper; read the poem again; and read and mark the paper again.

Large Scale Feedback:
Directions: Read your partner's paper silently and record all of your responses in writing before discussing your comments with the writer. Write clearly in complete sentences, using arrows and other markings to connect your feedback to specific text. Use the following questions as your guide to making comments.

Can readers understand what the poem is about even if they aren't deeply familiar with it? If not, let the writer know that he or she needs to strengthen the summary, so readers can get a handle on the poem.

Does the writer organize his or her explication in a way that makes sense to someone who is generally familiar with the poem? Is it organized from beginning to end? If not, does the organization make sense, or does the reader have to skip around a lot? Suggest a new plan for organization if necessary.

Do paragraph breaks make sense where they are? What seems to guide the writer's decision to make a new paragraph? Take each paragraph and imagine it stands alone. To someone familiar with the poem, does the paragraph make sense as a stand-alone? In other words, is the thought complete? Do the claim and the evidence and explanations that support it come through as clear and fully cooked?

Does the writer back up claims with evidence? Look for textual support for each and every claim. The support can be in the form of quote, summary, or paraphrase.

Small Scale Feedback:
Look at the opening paragraph and one other paragraph of your choice. Then using the Describing Text Templates, analyze large claims and subclaims and get down to the nitty-gritty of whether the writer is constructing valid interpretations and presenting those interpreted meanings effectively in his or her writing. Be sure to use the common language of the Describing Text Templates and write very specific questions and comments on your writer's paper.

If you happen to see repeated errors in spelling, punctuation, or sentence structure, please note them, but don't focus solely on conventions at this point. You may also suggest having the writer take a look at things that seem off, even if you aren't sure why they seem wrong to you.

Handout 11.A. Getting Ready to Recite: "Beat! Beat! Drums!"

Whether this is performed as an antiwar poem or a recruitment poem, it is a volatile piece. The intensity of this performance requires endurance on the part of the performer. It also requires careful strategizing regarding pace, volume, and pitch. Remember, as you practice saying each word, that silence or a whisper can sometimes be as powerful as a shout.

Step 1: Practice Breathing and Articulating
Say each word of the poem separately. Make sure that every sound of every word is clearly heard. The percussive qualities of the poem must be savored in a performance.

Step 2: Examine Multiple Intonations
After examining the poem's sentences and the lines, in two separate analyses, read the poem out loud as a recruitment poem, then as an antiwar poem. Examine the ways in which line break might contribute to both ways of reading it. Ultimately, you must determine which speech-act the speaker is performing at any given point in the poem. Is he or she commanding, explaining, accusing? Map it out and determine how your voice and gestures will convey your interpretation.

Step 3: Identify the Build, Crisis, Climax, and Dénouement
Now bring your knowledge of the poem to bear on your character and consider this question: How does the speaker feel about war? Commit to an interpretation (for or against) and build your recitation around it, looking for key parts such as line break, imagery, and speech act along the way.

Build—Background information about the situation.
Crisis—Turning point or change of idea that sets us up for the climax.
Climax—The most intense moment of the poem.
Dénouement—The unraveling that leads us back down from the peak and gives us closure.

360 Degrees of Text: Using Poetry to Teach Close Reading and Powerful Writing by Eileen Murphy Buckley © 2011 NCTE.

Handout 11.B. Sample Explication:
"Beat! Beat! Drums!" (1861) by Walt Whitman

How do poets create varying forms of speech acts as they compose sentences and lines within a poem?

With overwhelming images of destruction and pounding rhythms, Whitman's famous war poem mimics the fervent speech of a warmonger and leaves the reader nearly chanting in protest of war. Whitman catalogues the ways in which war obliterates peaceful domesticity, civil society, and even the restfulness of death in three powerful stanzas.

In the first stanza, Whitman's stressed, single-syllable words are interrupted only by the disyllabic "bugles." Each word in the line almost literally beats like the drums of war. The series of commands, which moves readers through a set of images representing the destruction of organized society—a church, a school, the nuptial bed—closes with the end of peace for the farmer at work. The once peaceful farmer is haunted by the "whirr" and "pound" of drums and "shrill" bugles that appear to sound without human agents.

While each of these images is encapsulated in a kind of military order, the line breaks allow for multiple ways of intoning this last line "So fierce you whirr and pound you drums—so shrill you bugles blow." As a separate unit of meaning, this line could be read not only as part of this list of military orders, but as an explanation for the crushing devastation.

With military regularity, the structure of the first stanza is repeated in the second stanza, but a question rather than a command becomes the dominant speech act. The very form of a question suggests an uncertain and, therefore, often more ominous menace. Playing on the terror of anticipation, the speaker threatens not only the action but also the speech that takes place in the emblematic spaces of civil society—the bedroom, the marketplace, the courtroom. The stanza closes, once again with the pounding command addressed to the inhuman yet animated instruments of war—"Then rattle quicker, heavier drums — you bugles wilder blow."

By associating speech acts with characters found among the earlier images, the final stanza maps back to the previous two and comments upon the most ominous of all threats, the diminished performative power of the human voice. The key words "parley" "expostulation," "prayer," and "beseeching" suggest that the drums of the final stanza threaten the power of human speech to stop the destruction, as in the line "Let not the child's voice be heard, nor the mother's entreaties." Whitman describes a world in which the power of human words has been annihilated by these now self-motivated drums. In the last image, "Make even the trestles to shake the dead, where they lie awaiting the hearses," even the sleep of death will be made impossible by the drums birthed by war. The powerful cadence of this series of iconic images, onomatopoeic devices, and chilling utterances gathers enormous weight in performance. Exploring repetition, line break, and other structural devices employed by the poet allows readers to discover the many possibilities for intoning the sentences of this poem.

continued on next page

Teaching Notes: Sample Explication of "Beat! Beat! Drums!"
The following sentences, taken from the sample, illustrate how important verb choice can be in a sentence of an academic essay, particularly literary analysis. The sample sentences illustrate the ways in which a writer's verb choice is itself part of the argument. Have students label each claim type on their handout.

(The agents of action are underlined and the actions themselves are in bold type.)

Sample Claim Sentence Describing the Writer's Choice

> <u>Whitman</u> **catalogues** the ways in which war **obliterates** peaceful domesticity, civil society, and even the restfulness of death in three powerful stanzas.

The word "lists" could have easily worked here, but "catalogues" suggests the enormity of Whitman's list, just as the word "obliterates" suggests the *total* destruction war causes. In choosing these verbs, the explicator argues that the poet's choices are purposeful, that they indeed have the effect the explicator is describing.

Sample Evidence Sentence Describing a Text as the Agent of Action

> The <u>series</u> of commands, which **moves** readers through a <u>set</u> of images **representing** the destruction of organized society—a church, a school, the nuptial bed, **closes** with the end of peace for the farmer at work.

This sentence describes the type of speech act Whitman has employed in the stanza (commands). It also summarizes the stanza's imagery. Note that the text—the speaker's words—is the agent of action in this sentence, not the author, not the speaker. It is the "series of commands" and the "set of images" that **move**, **represent**, and **close**. These verbs argue that the text itself calls for a specific interpretation of Whitman's imagery. I always point out that there is no reason for an explicator to say, "I think Whitman chose these images in order to suggest . . ." The explicator's verb choice in the description of that imagery asserts that argument already.

Sample Evidence Sentence Summarizing Actions in a Text

> <u>The once peaceful farmer</u> **is haunted** <u>by the</u> "whirr" and "pound" of drums and "shrill" bugles that **appear to sound** without human agents.

Again the verb phrases "is haunted" and "appear to sound" make claims about specific interpretations of Whitman's imagery. The interpretive description gives agency to the <u>sounds</u> and the <u>instruments</u> that make them.

Handout 11.C. Verbs for Describing Texts

This list is taken from the sample sentences in professional criticism. The list is not meant to be exhaustive; rather, it is just a beginning list that illustrates the variety of verbs available to academic writers who make arguments about all sorts of texts. These verbs can be used to describe *actions,* which can be performed by *a writer, a speaker, or an element of the text.*

Allows	Examined	Preclude
Announces	Exemplifies	Rationalize
Appears	Expected	Reads
Appreciates	Fashions	Recognize
Argues	Find	Reformulates
Asserts	Focused	Remarks
Assumes	Forces	Remind
Becomes	Goes on to tell	Retains
Brings out the nature	Grows	Says
Calls	Illuminates	Seem
Carries	Imagine	Signifies
Catalogue	Imitate	Situated
Certifies	Immerses	Speaks
Claims	Include	Speaks to
Continues	Inscribed	Specifies
Contrasts	Introduces	States
Correct	Keep	Straddles
Declares	Laid out	Struggle
Demonstrates	Leaves	Suggests
Describes	Locate	Takes
Displays	Makes (readers)	Takes on
Draws	Makes reference to	Takes place
Emphasizes	Mirrors	Tells
Enables	Moved	Tended
Engaged	Mused	Underlines
Entails	Noted	Warns
Establishes	Observed	Wonder
Evokes	Offers	Writes

360 Degrees of Text: Using Poetry to Teach Close Reading and Powerful Writing by Eileen Murphy Buckley © 2011 NCTE.

Handout 12.A. Independent Study Reflection

Directions: Answer the following questions in complete sentences.

What strategies (three or more) did you use in your close reading? Consider visualization, paraphrase, division into parts, SOAPSTone, read-aloud, think-aloud, form analysis, verb analysis, others.

What led to this choice? (past success, seemed appropriate for the poem, etc.)

How did you employ these strategies? Did you draw, speak out loud, rewrite, annotate, etc.?

Which were the most fruitful with this particular poem? Did any seem fruitless with this text?

Write a brief summary of the poem and construct a draft of a large claim about the poem. You may use notes, handouts, and original and sample explications to complete this process.

360 Degrees of Text: Using Poetry to Teach Close Reading and Powerful Writing by Eileen Murphy Buckley
© 2011 NCTE.

Handout 12.B. Explication Outline

Directions: Using the following outline, develop supporting sentences to complete the paragraphs in this brief explication. The challenge of this assignment is developing evidence-based arguments to support the claims made in each topic sentence, while indicating how each paragraph supports the overall claim.

By focusing on key elements of the text and exploring those key elements in each part of the poem, this writer has developed the framework for the entire argument. Your job is to prove it!

Larger Claim

In "Freeway 280" by Lorna Dee Cervantes, the speaker explores the tensions between modern American life and her Mexican cultural heritage.

In the first stanza, Cervantes illustrates this conflict by using elements of imagery and language.

The tension is heightened in the second stanza as she uses these key elements in her descriptions of the natural world, which, like her own Chicana identity, thrives despite attempts to conceal it.

By the end of the poem, the speaker resolves to return to her community to find out if the fragile connection she feels with this community is dead or merely dormant.

360 Degrees of Text: Using Poetry to Teach Close Reading and Powerful Writing by Eileen Murphy Buckley © 2011 NCTE.

Handout 12.C. Sample Student Explications

Sample—First Draft Explication of "Freeway 280" by Lorna Dee Cervantes

In Freeway 280, Lorna Dee Cervantes is attempting to convey her maturing process through descriptive diction, imagery and mixed language use. As she describes the setting she lived in the reader gets a sense of how she feels about her time, probably her teenage years or childhood, living near the freeway.

Cervantes begins the poem by providing the setting. Spanish is used to illustrate her origins, and the culture she is surrounded by, and the gray cannery gives a sense of sadness and poverty. But she assures the reader there was love and life in these depressing settings, portraying roses and geraniums. However she returns to a sad tone with an abrupt "are gone now". It seems as though she is returning to her old home, her casita, and remembering the "wild abrazos", hugs, of "climbing roses" where she used to live. Nestling and climbing have family and tradition connotations. The climbing roses give a sense of age and the little houses are nestled just as Cervantes was nestled in her family. The word "conceal" and "scar" have negative connotations, and Cervantes lets the reader know that the "abrazos" and roses have been removed for the freeway. As though the freeway has taken part of her away and scarred her, or scarred the whole land, that it is raised above. This is probably a comment on modernization or suburbanization, and the loss of her childhood roaming grounds. The imagery created by hugging and climbing roses puts the reader right into the casitas, seeing the sad gray cannery, surrounded by roses. A sense of happiness is reached and then pulled away by the freeway. The reader is meant to come to the same negative conclusions about the freeway as Cervantes has.

The following paragraph is also full of imagery, and attractive Spanish and English diction. Showing that there is new life and even though the fields have been trampled by lots and freeway structures, there are some greens poking through. "Wild mustard remembers" is an example of great verb selection to show that the new weeds remember the greatness of the old gardens, and the Spanish names for all the vegetables and fruits that Cervantes enjoyed when she was younger. Spanish names help to distinguish them as prepared in a Spanish fashion, and better illustrate the cultural influence on Cervantes childhood, a time when food is more important than most things.

The third paragraph is a moving picture. The center of Cervantes story too. She thinks of climbing the fence, and returning to what she has lost, and to what she used to want to escape from. She creates the image of her realization that although she used to want to leave on the "rigid lanes", which she calls rigid because they are so unnatural, she misses the smells and appeals to the readers pathos and tries to give them a feel for even such a detail as the texture of the air. The fence is closing off her old life, and she tries to scramble in, but she "scrambles" because its never easy to return to the past when the place the past once was is a lot under a highway.

The poem ends with her life-or-death assessment of the world outside her small home region by Freeway 280. She uses Spanish to illustrate that her home is a small farm, far from the city, because that home is probably a Latin American neighborhood and to her that means more than just language. Her culture is in her town. Her religion, her friends, her family and her way of life, gathering food beneath the "raised scar" of the freeway. This is all part of her heritage, living in heavily Mexican and South Ameri-

continued on next page

can California. She is speaking as though she were a young girl, impatient about her future and constantly reminded of the cities that cause all the traffic above her. Mown is, I believe, a reference to the cars above, mowing by on the freeway. "Mown" is chosen because they don't dawdle, they cruise and they speed to their destination. It's a symbol of the fast pace of the city. "Mown" is also meant to mean the mowing as of grass, and as she looks around below the freeway she is looking for part of herself, her childhood. Her words perfectly show that this part of her is either dead, like a corpse, or just a loose seed, yet to grow.

Through the images of where the small houses once were to the modern smells of pollution from passing cars, Cervantes constructs a setting of what was once her home. Her language brings out her culture in the picture of her old farm, and it becomes easy to visualize a demoralizing change of scenery. With these images in mind, the reader finds out that Cervantes misses her home, can see it, and hopes to be reconnected, hopes that the part of her that was mown under Freeway 280, can resurface like a loose seed rather than a corpse.

Aidan, Grade 11

Sample with Teacher Comments

Dear Aidan, you have done an excellent close reading and pointed out really interesting themes. I would like to see a revision. I love your focus on diction, imagery and mixed language use. I'd like you to work on organizing your comments about each of the techniques in a more chronological approach to the poem. Topic sentences might indicate new developments in the emotional drama, while the specific techniques that you point out can be discussed in the context of those topic sentences. After you work on the organization, you can start to fill in some of the associated meanings that are connecting the text to ideas outside the text in your mind. My comments should indicate where many of those are.

In Freeway 280, Lorna Dee Cervantes is attempting to convey her maturing process through descriptive diction, imagery and mixed language use. As she describes the setting she lived in the reader gets a sense of how she feels about her[1] time, probably her teenage years or childhood, living near the freeway.

[1] What do you mean by her time?

Cervantes begins the poem by providing details about the setting. Spanish is used to illustrate[2] her origins, and the culture she is surrounded by, and the gray cannery gives a sense of sadness and poverty.[3] But she assures the reader there was love and life in these depressing settings, portraying roses and geraniums.[4] However she returns to a sad tone with an abrupt "are gone now". It seems as

[2] Illustrate?

[3] Could this be a separate idea?

[4] How do you know this portrays love and life? Explain your associated

continued on next page

though she is returning to her old home, her casita, and remembering the "wild abrazos", hugs, of "climbing roses" where she used to live. Nestling and climbing have family and tradition connotations. The climbing roses give a sense of age and the little houses are nestled just as Cervantes was nestled in her family. The word "conceal" and "scar" have negative connotations, and Cervantes lets the reader know that the "abrazos" and roses have been removed for the freeway. As though the freeway has taken part of her away and scarred her, or scarred the whole land, that it is raised above. This is probably a comment on modernization or suburbanization, and the loss of her childhood roaming grounds. The imagery created by hugging and climbing roses puts the reader right into the casitas, seeing the sad gray cannery, surrounded by roses. A sense of happiness is reached and then pulled away by the freeway. The reader is meant to come to the same negative conclusions about the freeway as Cervantes has.[5]

The following paragraph[6] is also full of imagery, and attractive[7] Spanish and English diction. Showing that there is new life and even though the fields have been trampled by lots and freeway structures, there are some greens poking through. "Wild mustard remembers" is an example of great verb selection to show that the new weeds remember the greatness of the old gardens, and the Spanish names for all the vegetables and fruits that Cervantes enjoyed when she was younger.[8] Spanish names help to distinguish them as prepared in a Spanish fashion, and better illustrate the cultural influence on Cervantes childhood, a time when food is more important than most things.[9]

The third paragraph is a moving picture. The center of Cervantes story too.[10] She thinks[11] of climbing the fence, and returning to what she has lost, and to what she used to want to escape from. She creates the image of her realization[12] that although she used to want to leave on the "rigid lanes", which she calls rigid because they are so unnatural, she misses the smells and appeals to the readers pathos and tries to give them a feel for even such a detail as the texture of the air. The fence is closing off her old life, and she tries to scramble in, but she "scrambles" because its never easy to return to the past when the place the past once was is a lot under a highway.[13]

meanings here.

[5] This whole section focuses on imagery, but it jumps around a lot in terms of the chronology of the poem. Is there a way to divide the poem by the turns the emotional drama takes and discuss section by section, how the imagery reveals that drama? A couple of new topic sentences and a lot of copying and pasting might go a long way here to help the reader understand your train of thought.

[6] Do you mean section of the poem? Which one? Is there another way of indicating which section of the poem you are referring to?
[7] Best adjective in the context of your argument?

[8] Can you complete this thought, explaining why Cervantes may have included these particular details?
[9] Is this the only or most relevant significance in the context of your argument?
[10] Combine sentences?
[11] Now or then?

[12] How? Spell this out?

[13] Confusing wording here, and also, is there a metaphorical meaning to be explained?

continued on next page

The poem ends with her life-or-death[14] assessment of the world outside her small home region by Freeway 280. She uses Spanish to illustrate that her home is a small farm, far from the city, because that home is probably a Latin American neighborhood and to her that means more than just language.[15] Her culture is in her town. Her religion, her friends, her family and her way of life, gathering[16] food beneath the "raised scar" of the freeway. This is all part of her heritage, living in heavily Mexican and South American[17] California. She is speaking as though she were a young girl, impatient about her future and constantly reminded of the cities that cause all the traffic above her. Mown is, I believe, a reference to the cars above, mowing by on the freeway. "Mown" is chosen because they don't dawdle, they cruise and they speed to their destination. It's a symbol of the fast pace of the city. "Mown" is also meant to mean the mowing as of grass, and as she looks around below the freeway she is looking for part of herself, her childhood. Her words perfectly show that this part of her is either dead, like a corpse, or just a loose seed, yet to grow.[18]

Through the images of where the small houses once were to the modern smells of pollution from passing cars, Cervantes constructs a setting of what was once her home. Her language brings out her culture in the picture of her old farm,[19] and it becomes easy to visualize a demoralizing change of scenery. With these images in mind, the reader finds out that Cervantes misses her home, can see it, and hopes to be reconnected, hopes that the part of her that was mown under Freeway 280, can resurface like a loose seed rather than a corpse.[20]

[14] How so?

[15] Evidence?

[16] Who is performing this action?

[17] The part of California that was once Mexico?

[18] This is where you have a lot of interesting thoughts all jumbled together, like the other paragraph. You need to slow down here and spell things out, perhaps taking the poem more chronologically and tying your noticings about imagery and word choice into your discussion of each part of the drama.

[19] ?

[20] excellent ending

Revised Sample Explication of "Freeway 280" by Lorna Dee Cervantes
In Freeway 280, Lorna Dee Cervantes is attempting to convey her fading childhood memories through descriptive diction, imagery and mixed language use. As she describes the setting she lived in, the reader gets a sense of how she feels about her past.

Cervantes begins the poem by reminiscing about the visual setting of the freeway. She uses Spanish to give a sense of her origins, and the culture she was surrounded by in her childhood. The gray cannery gives a sense of sadness and poverty. But then she assures the reader there was love and life in these depressing settings. She does this by contrasting the cannery with roses and geraniums, which usually represent love and happiness. Flowers and fauna in general represent life. Nestling and climbing have connotations of family and tradition. The climbing roses give a sense of age and the little houses are nestled just as Cervantes was nestled in her Latin American community.

continued on next page

However she returns to a sad tone with the line beginning, "are gone now". It seems as though she is returning to her old home, her casita, and remembering the "wild abrazos", hugs, of "climbing roses" where she used to live.

The words "conceal" and "scar" have negative connotations, and Cervantes lets the reader know that the "abrazos" and roses have been removed for the freeway. It is as though the freeway has taken part of her away and scarred her, or scarred the whole land, that it is raised above. This is probably a comment on modernization or suburbanization, and the loss of her childhood roaming grounds.

The imagery created by hugging and climbing roses puts the reader right into the casitas, seeing the sad gray cannery, surrounded by roses. A sense of happiness is reached and then pulled away by the freeway. The reader is meant to come to the same negative conclusions about the freeway as Cervantes has.

The next stanza is also full of imagery and Spanish, and gives a sense of Cervantes' nostalgia. The stanza describes things she misses, but more how she feels that things have changed. "Wild mustard remembers" is an example of verb selection that makes the scene more meaningful. Cervantes means that wild mustard is one of the few recognizable plants left that were there when she was a child and there was no freeway. The mustard is personified to share the memory of the gardens she remembers. That is, the gardens full of all the Spanish plants she lists with sentimentality, shown by the ellipses, which give a sense of drifting off from the present to fond memories.

The description of the freeway at the beginning of the stanza is important because it shows the reader that Cervantes is not seeing the gardens, but rather the freeway. So she is not quite enthusiastic when she sees the scene she is laying out for the reader, but rather observant of changes and nostalgic for the faded past.

The third stanza is the center of Cervantes' story, as she returns to her origins and reveals her memory of wanting to leave the place she is speaking so fondly of. She imagines, or possibly remembers, climbing the fence that once sealed her in. She "scrambles" over because scrambling infers trouble, and it is a metaphor because Cervantes is having trouble breaking back into her past. She writes that she used to desire to be free from the farms when she was little, but now looking back she misses the farms. She even goes so far as to describe the specific smell of burning tomatoes, a scent she associates with the home she wanted to leave. She is being nostalgic about wanting to leave as she returns, or metaphorically returns, to the place of her childhood. At the time she wanted to exchange the scents she grew used to for somewhere new, but now looking at the weeds under the freeway, she recalls her childhood with fondness. She is explaining her realization that she loves and misses the time she spent where the freeway now stands, even though she wanted to let the freeway take her away while she was there.

The poem ends with Cervantes' final thought about her childhood. She is looking for the lost part of her in the place where that part of her lived, in English "the farms far from this city." She says it in Spanish, however, to point out her origins, and that it was not an English farm, it was one full of Latin American culture. But she has moved on from the old days: that's why she says "this city". But she wants to remember those days, so she metaphorically goes searching under the freeway for herself. And she searches, but she feels her past is "mown under" by the freeway, because none of the farmland is there, it is just a fenced off region under the "raised scar." The metaphor is that her old life is the corpse or the loose seed. Her diction perfectly shows that this part

continued on next page

of her is either dead, like a corpse, or just a loose seed, yet to grow. She includes a very vivid image of a fenced in region of weeds and wild mustard under the freeway where she is looking for a corpse or a seed that holds the little girl in her.

Through the images of where the small houses once were to wild mustard, Cervantes constructs a setting of what was once her home. Her language brings out her culture in the picture of her old farm, and it becomes easy to visualize the demoralizing change of scenery. With these images in mind, the reader finds out that Cervantes misses her home, can see it, and hopes to be reconnected. She hopes that the part of her that was mown under Freeway 280, can resurface like a loose seed rather than a corpse.

360 Degrees of Text: Using Poetry to Teach Close Reading and Powerful Writing by Eileen Murphy Buckley © 2011 NCTE.

Teaching Aid 1. Presentation of Revision Homework

Sample first draft sentence:

Whitman <u>describes</u> the effect of war, <u>using</u> the images of destruction.

Revision Strategy: Name the Agent Accurately

- Often there is a difference between the speaker and the author. The speaker of a poem is not always the same persona as the author. Male poets, for example, have often written from the point of view of a woman.
- Be sure that you name the agent accurately—the author, the speaker, or the text itself.

Revised Sentence (Stage 1):

*The **speaker** <u>describes</u> the effect of war, <u>using</u> the images of destruction.*

Revision Strategy: Describe the Action Precisely

- "Describes" is fine. It is an accurate description of what the speaker does, but since the speaker has a certain way of describing the effects of war and certain purpose in doing so, a more elaborate description of the speaker's move and a more precise verb might work better.

Revised Sentence:

The speaker's selection of images vividly illustrates the destructive effects of war.

- This sentence argues, more powerfully, more purposefully, that the speaker's selection of imagery is one tool at work in the overall scheme of the poem. In this revision, the agent of action who is illustrating is no longer the author or the speaker, but "the speaker's selection of images." Now the argument is that the speaker, a persona with a particular agenda, is doing something on purpose, selecting images, for a reason. That is just the kind of argumentation literary analysis requires!

360 Degrees of Text: Using Poetry to Teach Close Reading and Powerful Writing by Eileen Murphy Buckley © 2011 NCTE.

Teaching Aid 2. Before and After:
Workshopping with Templates and Revising Verb Choice

While this explication needs further revision, this sampling shows how the focus on Describing Text Templates and on verb choice leads the writer to a richer, more focused paragraph.

Excerpt of Draft 1
The poem "Beat! Beat! Drum!" by Walt Whitman, starts out with using especially descriptive terms creating an illustration of what the battle was like in 1861 (the time of the poem). Through out the poem, Whitman drills into you with chilling and irritating words to describe how negatively the war was affecting its surroundings. In the first stanza he says, "Through the windows—through doors—burst like a ruthless force." I feel that this quote explains how the problem would follow you everywhere you went and show no mercy: the problem being the war. The war was defined to be like a wrecking-ball; in conclusion it annihilates anything in its path. By the end of the poem, Whitman expects the person who has read it to feel a sense of compassion and pity for the citizens who were forced to live during the time of combat.

Excerpt of Draft 2
The poem "Beat! Beat! Drum!" by Walt Whitman, starts out with using especially descriptive terms creating an illustration of what a battle was like. Throughout the poem, Whitman drills into you with chilling and irritating words to describe how negatively the war was affecting its surroundings.

The drums and the bugles are often repeated throughout the poem in order to remind the people how important it is to fight for our country. In the first stanza he orders the drums and bugles, "Through the windows—through doors—burst like a ruthless force." Whitman's image shows how the war should follow a person everywhere he or she goes and show no mercy. The war is compared to a wrecking-ball; it annihilates everything and anything in its path. The speaker decides to threaten the people into sharing a part in the battle by sharing these treacherous images.

Excerpt of Draft 3
The drums and the bugles are often repeated throughout the poem in order to remind the people how important it is to fight for our country. In the first stanza he orders the drums and bugles, "Through the windows—through doors—burst like a ruthless force." Whitman's image shows how the war should follow a person everywhere he or she goes and show no mercy. The war is compared to a wrecking-ball; it annihilates everything and anything in its path. The speaker uses these terrifying images to intimidate the people into doing their part in battle to end the war.

Works Cited

Abrams, M. H. *A Glossary of Literary Terms*. New York: Holt, 1988. Print.

Afflerbach, Peter, P. David Pearson, and Scot G. Paris. "Clarifying Differences between Reading Skills and Reading Strategies." *Reading Teacher* 61.5 (2008): 364–73. *ProQuest*. Web. 23 Mar. 2010.

Anderson, Lorin W., and David R. Krathwohl, eds. *A Taxonomy for Learning, Teaching, and Assessing: A Revision of Bloom's Taxonomy of Educational Objectives*. New York: Longman, 2001. Print.

Banks, William P. "Beginning at the End: Encouraging Literacy by Rethinking the Developmental Model of an Oral Interpretation Course." *Teaching English in the Two-Year College* 30.1 (2002): 48–59. Print.

Caldwell, JoAnne Schudt. *Reading Assessment: A Primer for Teachers and Tutors*. New York: Guilford, 2002. Print.

Chicago Public Radio. "Speak!" *Eight Forty-Eight*. Chicago Public Radio. WBEZ, Chicago, 4 Apr. 2006. Web. 2 June 2011.

"Common Core State Standards Initiative: The Standards: English Language Arts Standards." *Common Core State Standards Initiative*. Web. 2 July 2011.

Ellis, Lindsay, Ann Ruggles Gere, and L. Jill Lamberton. "Out Loud: The Common Language of Poetry." *English Journal* 93.1 (2003): 44–49. Web.

Frost, Robert. "Nothing Gold Can Stay." 1923. *Poets.org*. Academy of American Poets. Web. 5 Feb. 2010.

Goodson, F. Todd, and Lori Atkins Goodson. "You Oughta Use the Periods and Stuff to Slow Down: Reading Fluency through Oral Interpretation of YA Lit." *Voices from the Middle* 13.2 (2005): 24–29. Print.

Graff, Gerald. *Beyond the Culture Wars: How Teaching the Conflicts Can Revitalize American Education*. New York, Norton, 1992. Print.

———. *Clueless in Academe: How Schooling Obscures the Life of the Mind*. New Haven: Yale UP, 2003. Print.

Graff, Gerald, and Cathy Birkenstein. "A Progressive Case for Educational Standardization." *Academe* 94.3 (2008): 16–20. *ProQuest*. Web. 26 Mar. 2010.

———. *They Say/I Say: The Moves That Matter in Academic Writing*. 2nd ed. New York: Norton, 2010. Print.

Graff, Nelson. "Approaching Authentic Peer Review." *English Journal* 98.5 (2009): 81–87. Print.

Heaney, Seamus. *The Redress of Poetry: Oxford Lectures*. London: Faber, 1995. Print.

Hillocks, George, Jr. "Teaching Argument for Critical Thinking and Writing: An Introduction." *English Journal* 99.6 (2010): 24–32. Print.

Hirsch, Edward. "Metaphor: A Poet Is a Nightingale." *Poetry Foundation.org*. Poetry Foundation, n.d. Web. 9 Jan. 2010.

Hughes, Langston. "Harlem." 1951. *Poetry Foundation.org*. Poetry Foundation. Web. 5 Feb. 2010.

Ivey, Gay, and Douglas Fisher. *Creating Literacy-Rich Schools for Adolescents*. Alexandria: Association for Supervision and Curriculum Development, 2006. Print.

Jago, Carol. "Crash! The Currency Crisis in American Culture." *National Council of Teachers of English*. NCTE, Apr. 2009. Web. 31 Mar. 2010.

———. *With Rigor for All: Teaching the Classics to Contemporary Students*. Portland: Calendar Islands, 2000. Print.

Knoeller, Christian. "Imaginative Response: Teaching Literature through Creative Writing." *English Journal* 92.5 (2003): 42–48. Print.

Kohn, Alfie. "How to Create Nonreaders: Reflections on Motivation, Learning, and Sharing Power." *English Journal* 100.1 (2010): 16–22. Print.

Kuhn, Deanna. *Education for Thinking*. Cambridge: Harvard UP, 2005. Print.

Lewis, Todd V. *Communicating Literature: An Introduction to Oral Interpretation*. Dubuque: Kendall/Hunt, 2004. Print.

Michaels, Judy Rowe. "Reimagining Coleridge's 'Rhyme of the Ancient Mariner' through Visual and Performing Arts Projects." *English Journal* 99.2 (2009): 48–54. Print.

O'Connor, John S. "Playing with Subtext: Using Groucho to Teach Shakespeare." *English Journal* 88.1 (1998): 97–100. Print.

Ortlieb, Evan, Neva Cramer, and Earl Cheek Jr. "The Art of Reading: Dramatizing Literacy." *Reading Improvement* 44.3 (2007): 169–76. Web. 18 July 2011.

Padgett, Ron. *The Teachers & Writers Handbook of Poetic Forms*. New York: Teachers and Writers Collaborative, 2000. Print.

Pinsky, Robert. *The Sounds of Poetry: A Brief Guide*. New York: Farrar, 1999. Print.

Powell, Joseph, and Mark Halperin. *Accent on Meter: A Handbook for Readers of Poetry*. Urbana, NCTE, 2004.

Rodenburg, Patsy. *Speaking Shakespeare*. New York: Palgrave-Macmillan, 2004. Print.

Rubin, Joan Shelley. *Songs of Ourselves: The Uses of Poetry in America*. Cambridge: Belknap-Harvard UP, 2007. Print.

Scholes, Robert. *The Crafty Reader*. New Haven: Yale UP, 2001. Print.

———. *Textual Power: Literary Theory and the Teaching of English*. New Haven: Yale UP, 1985. Print.

Shields, J. Scott. "The Art of Imitation." *English Journal* 96.6 (2007): 56–60. Print.

Strunk, William, Jr., and E. B. White. *The Elements of Style*. 4th ed. Needham Heights: Allyn and Bacon, 2000. Print.

Tanner, Fran Averett. *Readers Theatre Fundamentals: A Cumulative Approach to Theory and Activities*. Topeka: Clark, 1993. Print.

Thomas, Pat. "Mining for Gems: The Making of Readers and Writers." *Voices from the Middle* 8.2 (2000): 26–33. Print.

Tufte, Virginia. *Artful Sentences: Syntax as Style*. Cheshire: Graphics LLC, 2006. Print.

VanDeWeghe, Rick. "Research Matters: Authentic Literacy and Student Achievement." *English Journal* 97.6. (2008): 105–8. Print.

Vendler, Helen H., ed. *The Art of Shakespeare's Sonnets*. Cambridge: Harvard UP, 1999. Print.

———. *Poems, Poets, Poetry: An Introduction and Anthology*. Boston: Bedford/St. Martin's, 2002. Print.

Wilhelm, Jeffrey D. *Action Strategies for Deepening Comprehension: Role Plays, Text Structure Tableaux, Talking Statues, and Other Enrichment Techniques That Engage Students with Text*. New York: Scholastic, 2002. Print.

———. *Reading Is Seeing: Learning to Visualize Scenes, Characters, Ideas, and Text Worlds to Improve Comprehension and Reflective Reading*. New York: Scholastic, 2004. Print.

———. *"You Gotta BE the Book": Teaching Engaged and Reflective Reading with Adolescents*. New York: Teachers College; Urbana: NCTE, 1997. Print.

Williams, Joseph. *Style: Lessons in Clarity and Grace*. 10th ed. Rev. Gregory G. Colomb. Boston, Longman, 2010. Print.

Williams, William Carlos. "The Red Wheelbarrow." 1962. *Poets.org*. Academy of American Poets. Web. 5 Feb. 2010.

Wormeli, Rick. *Fair Isn't Always Equal: Assessing and Grading in the Differentiated Classroom*. Portland: Stenhouse, 2006. Print.

Index

Author

Photo by Cathy Chouinard

Eileen Murphy Buckley is the director of curriculum and instruction for the Pershing Network in Chicago Public Schools. She has served more than 100 of Chicago's highest-performing schools in developing strategies for school improvement through systematic attention to teacher learning. Murphy Buckley has taught high school English for more than fifteen years in three high schools, including one she helped found, Walter Payton College Preparatory High School in Chicago. Throughout her career, she has worked closely with national organizations, including the National Council of Teachers of English, the National Endowment for the Humanities, and Facing History and Ourselves, to increase teacher capacity for teaching critical literacy skills in engaging ways. She is currently working with Chicago principals to improve literacy instruction and professional development opportunities for teachers.

This book was typeset in Palatino and Helvetica by Barbara Frazier.
Typefaces used on the cover are Copperplate Light and Minion Pro.
The book was printed on 50-lb. Opaque Offset paper by Versa Press, Inc.